The Reform of Qatar University

T0306948

Joy S. Moini, Tora K. Bikson, C. Richard Neu, Laura DeSisto

With
Mohammed Al Hamadi, Sheikha Jabor Al Thani

Foreword by
Sheikha Al Misnad

RAND-QATAR POLICY INSTITUTE

The research described in this report was conducted within RAND Education and the RAND-Qatar Policy Institute, programs of the RAND Corporation.

Library of Congress Cataloging-in-Publication Data

The reform of Qatar University / Joy S. Moini ... [et al.] ; with Mohammed Al Hamadi, Sheikha Jabor Al Thani.
    p. cm.
    Includes bibliographical references.
    ISBN 978-0-8330-4744-1 (pbk. : alk. paper)
    1. Jami'at Qatar. 2. Educational change—Qatar. I. Moini, Joy S.

    LG358.D38R44 2009
    378.5363—dc22

                                                    2009025069

Cover photo courtesy Qatar University

The RAND Corporation is a nonprofit research organization providing objective analysis and effective solutions that address the challenges facing the public and private sectors around the world. RAND's publications do not necessarily reflect the opinions of its research clients and sponsors. **RAND®** is a registered trademark.

Published 2009 by the RAND Corporation
1776 Main Street, P.O. Box 2138, Santa Monica, CA 90407-2138
1200 South Hayes Street, Arlington, VA 22202-5050
4570 Fifth Avenue, Suite 600, Pittsburgh, PA 15213-2665
RAND URL: http://www.rand.org/
To order RAND documents or to obtain additional information, contact
Distribution Services: Telephone: (310) 451-7002;
Fax: (310) 451-6915; Email: order@rand.org

Preface

Since the 1990s, the State of Qatar has been capitalizing on the country's extraordinary oil and gas wealth to launch economic and social reforms aimed at modernizing and diversifying the country's economy. Key to these reforms has been the improvement and expansion of Qatar's education system from kindergarten through the post-secondary level. As part of the overall effort to improve the country's educational offerings, in 2003 His Highness the Emir of Qatar mandated major reforms at Qatar University (QU), the nation's first and only public higher education institution. The Diwan Amiri engaged the RAND-Qatar Policy Institute (RQPI) to assist the University with reform of its major administrative and academic structures, policies, and practices.

This monograph summarizes that reform effort. The formal reform project lasted from October 2003 through January 2007, and began with intensive discussions about the mission of the University, the obstacles the University faced in trying to fulfill this mission, and strategies for overcoming these obstacles. After articulating a plan for reform, the University embarked on an implementation process that addressed every major area of University operations, including achieving institutional autonomy, improving University decisionmaking processes, revitalizing academic offerings, improving faculty quality and performance and student achievement, and strengthening the University community.

The fundamental principle of the reform effort was that the University itself had to plan and institute the reform. Outsiders acted only as advisors, sharing their experiences and offering suggestions. By design, RQPI's role was limited to assisting the University leadership in organizing and facilitating the reform effort.

In particular, RQPI helped the University to identify a handful of foreign experts in higher education who joined with senior members of the University to form a Senior Reform Committee (SRC) that advised the University President on reform matters. RQPI worked with University staff to organize meetings of the SRC and to set agendas for these meetings. Only the RQPI project leader was a member of the SRC, and his role was restricted to organizing and facilitating meetings. RQPI also assisted the University in creating a small secretariat to support the SRC by gathering background information, documenting SRC recommendations, and tracking reform actions. A small number of RQPI staff worked alongside University staff as a part of this secretariat. RQPI's contribution to the QU reform effort was primarily organizational and supportive, rather than analytic.

In its assigned roles, RQPI was well positioned to observe the reform process, to understand the reasons that certain decisions were made, and to note the extent to which reforms were implemented in the years immediately following the decision to reform. RQPI had no mandate, however, to dictate any changes to QU's policies and practices or to assess independently the success of particular reform measures.

These limitations on RQPI's role are reflected in this monograph. In this document, we limit ourselves to describing what happened and why. Defense of the particular reform path chosen and assessment of the success of the reform are tasks for other analysts, best undertaken in the future when reforms have been fully implemented (or not, as the case may be) and their effects can be observed from an analytically appropriate distance.

This monograph should be of interest to Qatar University faculty, staff, and students in search of an overview of the reform process and a summary of changes that have been made at the University. The monograph may also be of interest to education policymakers, researchers, and scholars in Qatar, in the Gulf region, and internationally who are working on policy reform, implementation, and organizational change in higher education.

This project was conducted under the auspices of the RAND-Qatar Policy Institute and RAND Education. RQPI is a partnership of the RAND Corporation and the Qatar Foundation for Education, Science, and Community Development. The aim of RQPI is to offer the RAND style of rigorous and objective analysis to clients in the greater Middle East. In serving clients in the Middle East, RQPI draws on the full professional resources of the RAND Corporation. RAND Education analyzes education policy and practice and supports implementation of improvements at all levels of the education system.

For further information on RQPI, contact the director, Bruce Nardulli. He can be reached by email at nard@rand.org; by telephone at +974-492-7400; or by mail at P.O. Box 23644, Doha, Qatar. For more information about RAND Education, contact the director, Susan Bodilly. She can be reached by email at bodilly@rand.org; by telephone at +1-703-413-1100, extension 5377; or by mail at RAND, 1200 South Hayes Street, Arlington, Virginia, 22202-5050.

More information about RAND is available at www.rand.org.

Contents

Figures and Tables

Figures

Tables

A Leap of Fate: Reforming Qatar University

Sheikha Al Misnad, Ph.D.
President of Qatar University

Why Reform?

The State of Qatar is a relatively new and emerging country that has been catapulted by fate into the limelight of international energy and business markets owing to its substantial natural gas reserves. This newly acquired status necessitated rapid development of Qatar's human resources to a level of competency that meets the technological, business, and industrial needs of the country while at the same time responds to the social and cultural challenges that are bound to accompany accelerated development.

As Qatar's first and only national institution of higher education, Qatar University was the natural reservoir of the human resources that would be needed to lead and carry out the development movement. Established over three decades ago as a teacher training institution, the University had expanded over time to encompass six colleges covering disciplines ranging from Islamic studies to engineering and business.

In their early stages, the University's academic, administrative, and financial structures did not differ markedly from those existing in the region, i.e., they were marked by highly centralized decisionmaking processes, overly bureaucratic administrative and financial operations, and traditional pedagogy and program offerings. The Emir of the State of Qatar, who is also the Supreme Head of the University, saw that traditional mode of operation as inappropriate and insufficient for meeting the challenges of the future. In response, he commissioned the RAND-Qatar Policy Institute in 2003 to conduct an in-depth examination of the conditions and resources needed to turn Qatar University into a model national university.

What, Where, When, How

While the need for reform was evident, the way to proceed was not at all apparent, and there seemed to be many more questions than answers for a clear path forward. What should be the focus of the reform? What would be its guiding vision? Most importantly perhaps, was *how* the transformation of the University would happen. Where should the massive reform effort start? At what pace could the changes be introduced to sustain momentum yet avoid burnout? Planning and implementing change demands the dedication of the University's leadership, faculty, and staff—the building blocks of this institution. For the reform effort to be a success, fundamental yet deeply challenging shifts would be required in deep-seated attitudes, long-held perspectives, and daily behaviours of all University members. This report is an account of decisions made, actions taken, and lessons learned by a joint Qatar University–RQPI team as it pursued an ambitious agenda of innovation.

Turning Dreams into Realities

Qatar University has taken steps unprecedented in the region to transform itself into an institution that is at the cutting edge of higher education philosophy and practice. To establish quality assurance, it took strategic steps to pursue academic accreditation for its programs from noted international accrediting agencies, including vigorous recruitment of a diverse and highly qualified workforce. A piece of that dream was realized when the engineering programs offered by the College of Engineering received Accreditation Board for Engineering and Technology (ABET) equivalency in 2005. The University is now working to realize this dream for its programs in business, the sciences, liberal arts, and education in the near future.

The coming three to five years are crucial for Qatar University. The meticulous planning and budgeting that have been invested in the reform effort are only equalled by the efforts of the University's faculty, administration, and staff. Qatar University, however, will face a major challenge in the foreseeable future—notably the challenge of transforming the work culture. We realize that, in order for our efforts to bear fruit and hold true meaning, we must change the previous culture of operation into one in which learning is student-centered, administration is decentralized, and the individual is held accountable for his or her actions. The leap of fate that catapulted the State of Qatar into the limelight must be matched by a quantum leap by Qatar University to play its role in providing qualified professionals. While only time will tell if our quantum leap succeeds, we will spare no effort to turn dreams into realities.

Summary

Introduction

In August 2003, His Highness Sheikh Hamad Bin Khalifa Al Thani, the Emir of Qatar, appointed a new President, Sheikha Al Misnad, and other senior officers of Qatar University (QU), giving the new administration a broad mandate to reform and to strengthen the University. In October 2003, the Diwan Amiri[1] engaged the RAND-Qatar Policy Institute (RQPI) to assist the new QU leadership in designing and implementing a major reform of the University. This monograph recounts the motivation for the reform effort, describes the design of the reform agenda, and details the early stages of the implementation effort, with an eye toward identifying challenges yet to be met.

The State of Qatar

Qatar is a small monarchy on the Arabian Peninsula approximately the size of the state of Connecticut, bordered only by Saudi Arabia, to the southwest. From 2004 to 2008, the population doubled from nearly 750,000 to some 1.5 million; however, only about 20 percent are Qatari nationals; the rest comprise expatriate workers and their families.

With the world's third largest natural gas reserves, Qatar is a prosperous country. Under the current Emir, Qatar has aggressively pursued modernization, including economic and social development. As part of these modernization efforts, major reforms of health care and education have been undertaken, the latter aimed, in part, at preparing

---

[1] The administrative office of the Emir.

Qataris to assume more of the professional positions formerly held by expatriates. "Qatarization" of professional jobs is a high priority.

Education in Qatar

Recognizing the need for a better-prepared workforce, the Emir has made reform and strengthening of education in Qatar a high priority since the early years of his rule and directed a number of initiatives aimed at improving educational opportunities for young Qataris.

The first of these initiatives—chronologically—was the creation of an Education City in Doha. Both a physical campus and an administrative apparatus, Education City hosts a variety of educational, research, and cultural institutions, including branch campuses of leading foreign universities. In addition, though not formally a part of Education City, other branch campuses that offer technical training and vocationally oriented education have been set up in Doha.

The second major education initiative in Qatar was the establishment of a system of state-funded "Independent schools" serving students eligible for state-supported K–12 education aimed at providing autonomy, accountability, variety, and choice for parents and students in Qatar. The first 12 Independent schools opened in the fall of 2004. Additional Independent schools have opened in each succeeding year.

The Education City branch campuses cannot accommodate—and were never intended to accommodate—the large majority of Qatari secondary school graduates who sought academically oriented higher education but did not qualify for or chose not to attend foreign universities. For these graduates, Qatar University was the traditional and still most appropriate option. By 2003, the need to strengthen QU to meet the needs of a new generation of young Qataris was apparent. The principal piece missing from Qatar's overall education reform agenda was the reform of Qatar University.

Qatar University

The institution that became Qatar University began in 1973 as a College of Education. The University was formally established by Emiri decree in 1977, and by 2003 had six colleges: Education; Humanities and Social Sciences; Science; Sharia, Law, and Islamic Studies; Engineering; and Business and Economics.

QU is a state institution, and the state provides the bulk of the resources necessary for its operation. Although the Emiri decree that established the University guaranteed its autonomy, this autonomy had never been achieved in practice. The University's budget allocations had to be approved by the Ministry of Finance, and organization charts, staffing plans, and personnel actions had to be approved by the Ministry of Civil Service Affairs and Housing.

At the beginning of the reform effort, the University enrolled a total of about 8,600 students, about three-quarters of whom were women. The University provided separate campuses for men and for women, and all classes and extracurricular activities were gender-segregated.

Each college of the University awarded bachelor's degrees in its areas of specialization, and two of the colleges offered postgraduate degrees. The language of instruction in three of the University's colleges—Engineering, Science, and Business and Economics—was English. The remaining three colleges taught in Arabic.

Admissions standards were also set separately by each college of the University. In effect, students were accepted by and subsequently enrolled in a particular college rather than in the larger University.

When the reform effort began in 2003, QU had about 400 faculty members. Although the University had no formal system of granting tenure, Qatari faculty members were, in effect, appointed for life. Expatriate faculty were usually on renewable one-year contracts. There was no formal appraisal system. Expatriate faculty members were paid less than Qatari faculty, and, relative to other universities in the Gulf region, salaries were low for all faculty.

Before the reform, the University operated five research centers established to conduct applied research.[2] But these centers were not

---

[2] The centers were the Scientific Applied Research Center, the Sira and Sunna Research Center, the Educational Research Center, the Documentation and Humanities Research Center, and the National Center for Economic Research.

closely affiliated with University's colleges, and academic and research activities were not well coordinated.

The Need for Reform

In its earlier years, Qatar University had been regarded by many observers—both inside and outside Qatar—as one of the better universities in the Middle East. By a number of measures, however, the University's performance had been deteriorating for several years before the reforms were launched. Among the most prominent problems were the lengthening time that students required to complete their degree programs and the growing fraction of graduating students who did so with very poor grades. Qualitative indicators of student engagement also suggested problems—particularly among male students. Anecdotal reports abounded of poor student class attendance, lackadaisical approaches to studies, and occasional hectoring of faculty by students or parents about grades. Few extracurricular activities were available to students. At the beginning of the reform effort, students, faculty, and administrators agreed that no University community existed in any meaningful sense.

By some objective measures, the quality of the faculty was also declining. Within a faculty of roughly constant size, the number of lecturers (as opposed to assistant professors and professors) was rising, and the number of full professors had fallen sharply in the years before the reform. More-qualitative measures also suggested problems with the faculty. Morale was widely reported to be low.

In the years leading up to the reform effort, the University's internal administration had become increasingly centralized. Faculty complained that the central administration was usurping authorities that had traditionally rested with the faculty and with academic departments. There was growing estrangement between the central administration and the faculty.

In 2003, the University had no written compilation of procedures documenting how important academic or administrative processes were to be conducted. Key aspects of University life were handled through sometimes inconsistent improvisation or governed by long-standing but unwritten tradition.

The University was also facing financial difficulties. In the decade before the reforms began, University funding had not kept pace with the rising numbers of students.

Finally and most importantly, evidence was accumulating by 2003 that the University was failing to meet the needs of the larger Qatari society. Employers in Qatar—in both the public and private sectors—reported that few University graduates met required standards for employment.

By the summer of 2003, then, reforms of some key elements of Qatar's educational system were well under way. Action in other parts of the Qatari educational system served to make the absence of reform in the national university increasingly conspicuous—especially since both objective and perceptual indicators of University performance had been deteriorating for several years. It was against this backdrop that a major overhaul of Qatar University was launched in the fall of 2003.

Designing the Reform Agenda

The fundamental principle guiding the reform effort was that QU itself—its leading faculty and administrators—had to initiate and lead the reform. The reasons were threefold: University faculty knew better than anyone else QU's strengths and weaknesses; successful reform depended on faculty and staff ownership of the effort; and a key objective was to imbue QU with the capacity for continuing self-assessment and adjustment. At the same time, the critical role of impartial outside experts was understood.

A Senior Reform Committee (SRC) comprising senior QU members and outside experts from top universities in the United States and United Kingdom served as a forum for discussion about QU's mission and helped shape reform proposals. A reform project staff composed of both QU and RQPI members served as secretariat to the SRC. The SRC set about articulating the objectives of the reform as well as the principal obstacles.

The SRC first defined the appropriate mission of QU. This mission included being the major post-secondary school option for qualified Qatari students, serving as the principal reservoir of knowledge and expertise for the developing state, setting standards for the nation's social development, recognizing intellectual expertise and achievement, promoting informed discussion of key issues facing the nation, and promoting understanding of these issues. The SRC also articulated the need for a core curriculum for all students in addition to the courses in their areas of specialization and emphasized that QU should remain primarily an undergraduate institution.

The SRC identified seven major impediments to the University fulfilling its mission: inadequate administrative infrastructure, excessive administrative centralization, failure of academic and administrative structures to keep pace with changing educational demands and trends, lack of systematic academic planning, lack of cohesion among the individual academic programs, inadequate faculty quality, and lack of faculty commitment to QU's mission.

In the first year, the SRC proposed to the Emir a set of reforms consisting of seven recommendations:

1. Establish autonomy by creating a Board of Regents that would oversee the University.
2. Decentralize the administrative arrangements.
3. Modify the academic structure by unifying the colleges and integrating research and academic activities.
4. Institute a core curriculum for all students.
5. Introduce university-wide academic planning.
6. Improve the management of faculty and staff by improving compensation, linking pay with performance, and introducing tenure and other reforms.
7. Foster and support student achievement by enforcing admission standards and expanding services for students.

The recommendations were presented to the Emir with a set of specific requests, which he approved. Implementation began immediately.

Implementing the Reform Agenda

One of the biggest challenges to implementing the changes was the bureaucratic structure that was in place at the beginning of the reform. The first step in the reform effort was to restructure QU's administration to create university self-governance.

Noteworthy in the reform effort is the time frame in which most of the reforms were completed and the fact that each of the recommended reform initiatives has either been completed or is in progress. To assess further the success of the initiative, the SRC recommended developing and implementing a prospective evaluation system to track performance improvement.

Reflections on the Reform Strategy

The reforms proposed for Qatar University were extensive, touching virtually every constituency in the University community. In retrospect, several factors or conditions made such sweeping reform possible:

- *Timing of the reform.* The effort took advantage of the momentum created by the social, economic, educational, and governmental transformation in process in the country.
- *Organization and sequencing of reform.* Organization of the effort into distinct phases allowed for modular completion of activities and created milestones for measurement of progress as well as opportunities for reflection.
- *Strong leadership.* The leadership of QU's president as well as the recruitment and retraining of strong college, department, and program directors was critical.
- *University as the primary actor.* Recognition of the need for QU to reform itself and the coordination of activities by the internal Office of Institutional Planning and Development were key to progress.
- *Support from outside experts.* Strong trusting relationships were formed with the external advisors and technical consultants, who acted as sounding boards.

Nevertheless, designing and implementing the reform agenda involved difficult choices:

- *Academic standards versus social norms.* Faced with preserving the status quo, in which a university education was available to all nationals, or upholding academic standards, the administration decided that QU would uphold its new standards and aim to serve average and above-average students, while expanding its preparatory Foundation Program.
- *Pragmatism versus ambition.* The SRC recommended that QU aspire to goals that could realistically be achieved in a few years while making provisions for more ambitious expansion later.
- *Well-established versus innovative academic structures.* Rather than attempting a more innovative academic structure that would involve combining the Colleges of Science and Engineering, the QU leadership chose the more traditional path of creating a College of Arts and Sciences, with responsibility for delivering the core curriculum as well as its own programs.
- *University service versus scholarly development.* Faced with the difficult decision of whether to assign a number of promising young faculty members to key administrative positions or to allow them to pursue and build their own academic careers, QU's president had little choice but to assign them to the leadership positions, with the hope that they might eventually be able to return to teaching and research.
- *Rapid versus gradual reform.* The rapid pace of reform had the advantage of creating a self-perpetuating momentum and leaving little time for opposition. However, the University paid a price for proceeding so rapidly, as the result was considerable confusion and some resistance to change.
- *Efficiency versus inclusiveness.* Likewise, faced with the choice of trying to bring the entire faculty along at once (some of whom resisted change) or enlisting a growing circle of respected faculty who were supportive of change, the President chose the latter alternative. Although her decision did not ensure unanimity of views

and had its costs (some faculty felt disenfranchised and some left QU), the QU leadership does not regret this choice.

The Challenges Ahead

Since the launch of QU's reforms in 2003, the academic infrastructure, programs, and policies envisioned in the original reform agenda have already undergone some adjustment. However, these adjustments have originated from within the newly autonomous university without deferring to outside authorities or relying on outside assistance.

Several tests remain for the reformed university:

- At present, the most pressing academic challenge remains the completion of the core curriculum.
- The next major test for the reforms will occur when the current administration is replaced by the next generation of leaders.
- It remains possible that the university's autonomy may be tested by demands placed on it by the state, which provides the bulk of the financial resources on which the university depends.
- Finally, and more broadly, the university must complete the realignment of faculty and student attitudes, expectations, and behaviors that the reform has begun. This realignment is beginning to be felt in a new acceptance of accountability and recognition of individual responsibility, but it is something that must emerge over time and cannot be enforced from the top.

The QU reforms have brought changes in the structure and organization of the University. They have also prompted the beginnings of change in the less formal and less easily controlled spirit of the University. Completing these latter changes and making them enduring are the challenging tasks that QU must confront in the coming years.

Acknowledgments

The authors are grateful for the invaluable contributions of the Senior Reform Committee (SRC) members who served the University over the three years of the reform project: Omar Al Ansari, Roger Benjamin, Humaid Al Midfaa, Sheikha Al Misnad, Kenneth Keller, Jane Lightfoot, Marvin Peterson, Daniel Resnick, Nabeel Al Salam, Noura Al Subaai, and Farris Womack. Their willingness to share their insights, experience, and time to strengthen Qatar University was remarkable.

We would like to thank our fellow project staff members, Abdulla Al Thani, Rae Archibald, Ahmed Baker, Abdul Aziz El Bayoumi, Hassan Al Fadala, Marla Haims, Yousef Al Horr, Hind Jolo, Rita Karam, Abdul Nasser Muhammed, Hamda Al Naemi, Jihane Najjar, Hassan Al Sayed, Ali Al Shaib, Mary Kim, Marc Chun, and Mie Al Missned, for their important contributions to the reform process and the spirit of collegiality and teamwork that they provided throughout the project. We would also like to thank Donna Betancourt for ensuring that the SRC meetings were well planned and executed.

We would also like to thank the faculty, staff, and students—too numerous to name individually—at Qatar University who participated in the reform project in many and diverse ways. Reform at Qatar University truly would not be possible without them.

Finally, this monograph benefited from constructively critical reviews by Bruce Nardulli, Senior Political Scientist at the RAND-Qatar Policy Institute, and Maryann Gray, Assistant Provost of the University of California, Los Angeles.

None of the individuals named or referenced above bear any responsibility for the factual accuracy of this monograph. We gained enormously from our interactions with them, but any inaccuracies or misjudgments that remain in this monograph, despite their efforts, reflect failings of the authors alone.

Abbreviations

CAS   College of Arts and Sciences

FPAS   Faculty Performance Appraisal System

GDP   gross domestic product

GPA   grade point average

IT   information technology

OIPD   Office of Institutional Planning and Development

QU   Qatar University

RQPI   RAND-Qatar Policy Institute

SRC   Senior Reform Committee

CHAPTER ONE

Introduction

In August 2003, His Highness Sheikh Hamad Bin Khalifa Al Thani, the Emir of Qatar, appointed a new President and other senior officers of Qatar University (QU). Acting in his capacity as the Supreme Head of the University, the Emir gave this new leadership a broad mandate to reform and strengthen the University. In October 2003, the Diwan Amiri engaged the RAND-Qatar Policy Institute (RQPI)[1] to assist the new QU leadership in designing and implementing a major reform of the University.

Late in 2003, the University formally began to craft a broad reform agenda. The Emir approved the proposed reforms in June 2004, and the University immediately set to work on implementing them. The process of reform within QU continues today and ideally will continue indefinitely. Consequently, no account of University reforms can ever be complete. Sufficient time has passed since the reform effort began, however, to allow a useful look backward at what has been accomplished at QU, why, and how.

This monograph explains the motivations for the reform effort, describes the processes through which the reform agenda took shape, summarizes the main elements of the reform program, and details

---

[1] RQPI is a partnership of the RAND Corporation and the Qatar Foundation for Education, Science, and Community Development. RAND is a not-for-profit organization headquartered in the United States and devoted to serving the public interest through research and education. Qatar Foundation is a not-for-profit entity based in Doha and dedicated to advancing the social development of Qatar. In September 2003, RQPI established a permanent office in Doha's Education City, staffed by experienced analysts from RAND's offices in the United States and selected staff hired locally.

the early stages of the University's implementation of the reform program. The remainder of this chapter provides a brief overview of social and economic conditions in the State of Qatar around the time that the QU reform was launched. In particular, we place the University reform within the context of broader educational reform efforts that were under way in the country at that time. We then describe QU as it was structured and operating on the eve of the reform and summarize the conditions that made reform an urgent matter.

Chapter Two describes the process by which the University arrived at a plan for reform. In particular, we detail the close collaboration between members of the University and outside advisors in designing the reform agenda. We stress that all parties recognized from the beginning that the University had to reform itself and that outside experts could play no more than an advisory role. This chapter also summarizes the reform plan that was presented to His Highness the Emir after some eight months of work. With His Highness's approval, this plan became the blueprint for a major restructuring of the University.

Chapter Three describes how the reform plan was implemented during the following two years. It provides an overview of each of the major areas of reform activity and summarizes the progress made.

Chapter Four offers some observations about conditions and circumstances that made reform possible. This chapter also highlights some difficult choices that the University leadership had to make in formulating and implementing the reform agenda and explains how the leadership found a workable path through these difficult choices.

The final chapter looks at the challenges that lie ahead for the University in institutionalizing the reform.

The State of Qatar

Qatar is a small country on the Arabian Peninsula. Its land area is 11,437 square kilometers (about the size of the U.S. state of Connecticut). Its only land border—to the southwest—is with Saudi Arabia. The capital is Doha.

An official census found the population of Qatar to be 744,029 in March 2004, just a few months after the effort to reform Qatar University began. Significantly, Qatari nationals accounted for only about one-fifth of the total population.[2] The remainder of the population was made up of expatriate workers and their families.[3] In the years since then, Qatar's population has grown rapidly, driven by a continuing influx of foreign workers. In early 2008, the Secretary General of Qatar's General Secretariat of Development Planning offered an "unofficial" estimate of Qatar's population of 1.5 million—a doubling of the population in just four years![4]

Qatar is a prosperous country, with the world's third largest proven reserves of natural gas (after Russia and Iran). Continuing development of the offshore North Gas Field has underpinned Qatar's high and rapidly growing gross domestic product (GDP). The World Bank estimates that in 2003, at the beginning of the University reform, Qatar's per capita GDP calculated at purchasing power parity exchange rates was the equivalent of $57,041, among the highest in the world (World Bank, 2009).[5] By 2005, Qatar's per capita GDP had risen to $70,716 on a purchasing power parity basis, the highest in the world. The Economist Intelligence Unit estimates Qatar's real GDP growth to have averaged just under 10 percent per year over the period 2003 through 2007 (Economist Intelligence Unit, 2008).

Qatar is a monarchy, with ultimate authority vested in the Emir. Under the terms of a new constitution approved in a 2003 referendum, a new Consultative Council will have authority to review and potentially to reject government-proposed budgets and legislation. The Council will also be able to propose legislation on its own authority. Although the Emir will continue to appoint cabinet ministers, the Council will have the power—by a two-thirds majority—to dismiss

---

[2]   See Planning Council, Government of Qatar, 2004.

[3]   Low-skilled expatriate workers—laborers (typically male) and domestic workers (typically female)—generally live in Qatar without their families. Expatriate professionals are typically accompanied by their families.

[4]   See "Bursting at the Seams," 2008.

[5]   By way of comparison, U.S. per capita GDP in 2003 was $37,750.

these ministers. Two-thirds of the seats in the Consultative Council will be filled through popular elections. The Emir will appoint the remaining one-third of the members. As of early 2009, the first elections for the Consultative Council had not yet taken place.[6]

Qatar has pursued aggressive programs of modernization, economic development, and social development since the current Emir came to power in 1995. Major building programs are bringing the country world-class structures, accommodation, and infrastructure. Entire new cities are rising around Doha. Steps are being taken to streamline the civil service and to encourage Qataris to seek employment in the private sector. Major reforms of education and health care have been launched. Women are playing an increasingly prominent role in the affairs of the country: Two women serve as cabinet ministers, and others serve as chairpersons of important government authorities and national institutions. Qatar is seeking to establish itself as a regional center of learning, culture, and high-level international gatherings. Qatar is also working to establish itself as a center for international sporting events. In 2006, Doha was the host city for the Fifteenth Asian Games, and Qatar was among the seven applicant cities that bid to host the 2016 Olympic Games.

Education in Qatar

All Qatari nationals and the children of expatriate government employees are entitled to free education through grade 12 in state-funded schools. Children of other expatriates in Qatar attend fee-charging private schools offering international curricula or curricula keyed to the educational standards of the various countries from which large numbers of expatriates come. High-quality private schools are also increasingly popular with Qatari parents, and, in the 2008–2009 academic year, the government began to underwrite a portion of tuition costs for some Qatari nationals who attend approved private schools. The gov-

---

[6]   Elections to a purely advisory "Municipal Council" have been conducted for several years.

ernment is also working actively to encourage establishment of additional private schools to serve both Qatari and expatriate families.

Qatari nationals who perform sufficiently well on national standardized school-leaving examinations are entitled to free higher education at the national university. The best performers, who qualify for state- or company-funded scholarships, may enroll at Western university branch campuses now operating in Qatar or at universities abroad. Young Qataris who do not qualify for scholarships may attend foreign universities at their own or their parents' expense as an alternative to enrolling in the national university.

As is the case with all countries open to the challenges and opportunities of the modern global economy, Qatar needs a strong educational system to prepare young Qataris for increasingly demanding careers and to play leading roles in the future development of their own society. Qatar's demographics and its considerable economic potential, however, make the need for educational reform more urgent than in most other countries. Because there are so few Qatari nationals, Qatar's rapid economic growth inevitably depends on the presence of large numbers of expatriate workers. Low-skilled foreign workers perform most of the onerous jobs in the construction and service sectors that are considered unsuitable for Qataris. But well-educated expatriates are also filling professional and managerial jobs that would be attractive to Qataris with appropriate education and job skills. "Qatarization" of these professional and managerial jobs is a high priority for the Qatari government.

Unfortunately, few Qataris today have the education and the skills to fill professional and managerial positions, particularly in the private sector. A 2004 survey found that 78 percent of employed Qatari nationals worked for the government and that another 20 percent worked for fully or partially state-owned companies. Only 2 percent of Qatari workers were employed in the truly private sector (Planning Council, Government of Qatar, 2005, p. 41). Government ministries and agencies are widely seen as overstaffed, yet efforts to streamline the civil service risk forcing many Qataris into the private sector, where they will find themselves poorly equipped to compete for good positions against better-educated and more experienced expatriates. Interviews with employers—both government and private—consistently evoke reports of how difficult it is to find Qataris with the technical skills, problem-solving capacity, pro-innovation orientation, and workplace attitudes necessary for success in an increasingly open and competitive economy (Stasz, Eide, and Martorell, 2007). In Qatar, successful educational reform is key to enabling governmental reform and to sustaining effective Qatari management of the nation's rapidly growing economy. The small population of Qatari nationals must be particularly well educated if they are to fill effectively the top managerial positions in the country. Without significant advances in the educational achievement of Qatari nationals, the tasks of managing the nation's economic (and perhaps social) development will be left, by default, to better-trained expatriates.

Recognizing the need for a better-prepared workforce, His Highness the Emir has made reform and strengthening of education in Qatar a high priority since the early years of his rule. A number of initiatives aimed at improving educational opportunities for young Qataris were already under way before the reform of Qatar University was launched.

The first of these initiatives—chronologically—was the creation of an Education City in Doha. Education City is the principal project of the Qatar Foundation for Education, Science, and Community Development, a not-for-profit, non-governmental body led by Her Highness Sheikha Mozah Bint Nasser Al Missned, the Consort of the Emir. Both a physical campus and an administrative organization, Education City hosts a variety of educational, research, and cultural institutions. A top priority of Qatar Foundation has been to attract branch campuses of leading foreign universities to Education City. By the 2003–2004 academic year, when the QU reform began, three American universities were operating branch campuses in Education City: Virginia Commonwealth University, Weill Cornell Medical College, and Texas A&M University. Three additional branch campuses have opened since then, operated, respectively, by Carnegie Mellon University, Georgetown University, and Northwestern University.

Each of these branch campuses offers degree programs—taught in English—in particular academic specializations. Each branch campus confers the same degree in Qatar as at its home campus, and each adheres to the same standards for admission and graduation as does the home campus. By the 2007–2008 academic year, all branch-campus programs were coeducational.[7]

These branch campuses provide high-quality education to the best of Qatari secondary school graduates and to qualified applicants from elsewhere in the region. Qatar Foundation has also established an Academic Bridge Program to provide supplementary preparation—in English, mathematics, computer literacy, and study skills—for Qatari secondary school graduates who aspire to enroll in one of the Education City branch campuses or in a foreign university.

Although not formally a part of Education City, a Canadian technical college, the College of the North Atlantic, opened a branch campus in Doha in 2003, replacing a state-run vocational college. Additionally, CHN University of the Netherlands offers bachelor's degree programs in hospitality-related fields and in business administration. In 2006, the options for post-secondary study widened further when the University of Calgary set up a four-year degree program in nursing.

The second major education initiative in Qatar was the establishment of a system of state-funded "Independent schools" serving students eligible for state-supported K–12 education. These schools operate under charters granted by the Supreme Education Council (SEC). They must adhere to curriculum standards set by the SEC in Arabic, English, math, science, and Islamic studies, but they enjoy more flexibility in staffing and choices of instructional materials and methods than do traditional state-funded schools managed by the Ministry of Education. The first 12 Independent schools opened in the fall of 2004, and additional Independent schools have opened in each succeeding year. The Independent schools constitute a new K–12 educational system operating in parallel to the Ministry of Education schools, and parents of children eligible for state-funded education can choose to send their children either to a traditional Ministry school or to an Independent school (Brewer et al., 2007).

---

[7] Prior to the 2007–2008 academic year, Virginia Commonwealth University's programs—in graphic, interior, and fashion design—had been open only to women.

Thus on the eve of the Qatar University reform, important pieces of an overall educational reform strategy were already in place in Qatar. Significant efforts were under way to improve the quality of K–12 education available to young Qataris. Branch campuses of high-quality and highly selective foreign universities were beginning to provide alternatives to foreign study for the best of Qatari secondary school graduates. The Academic Bridge Program was in place to help promising graduates who needed more preparation for study in Education City or abroad. Finally, new vocational options were available for young Qataris who did not wish to pursue an academic track in higher education.

The Education City branch campuses could not accommodate— and were never intended to accommodate—the large majority of Qatari secondary school graduates who sought academically oriented higher education but did not qualify for or chose not to attend foreign universities. For these graduates, Qatar University was the traditional and still most appropriate option. By 2003, the need to strengthen QU to meet the needs of a new generation of young Qataris was apparent. The principal piece missing from Qatar's overall education reform agenda was the reform of Qatar University.

Qatar University[8]

The institution that became Qatar University began in 1973 as a College of Education. The University was formally established by Emiri decree in 1977, when three additional colleges were created: the College of Humanities and Social Sciences; the College of Science; and the College of Sharia and Islamic Studies. By 2003, QU had six colleges: Education; Humanities and Social Sciences; Science; Sharia, Law, and Islamic Studies; Engineering; and Business and Economics.

---

[8]   Prior to the reform project, the institutional data available for QU was quite limited; therefore, the information provided in this section necessarily lacks the type of comprehensive statistical and historical profile that is typically available for many universities.

Governance

QU was and remains a state institution, and the state provides the bulk of the resources necessary for its operation. At the time the reforms began, QU had no high-level external oversight body. The Emir, in his capacity as Supreme Head of the University, constituted the principal outside authority over the University. The Emir had the power to appoint or to replace the President and other senior officials of the University. In earlier years, the University had a consultative (but non-governing) Board of Regents, but this Board was suspended in 1995.

Although the Emiri decree that established the University guaranteed its autonomy, this autonomy had never been achieved in practice. Allocations of the overall University budget to specific purposes had to be approved by the Ministry of Finance, as did any subsequent adjustments or reallocations in budgeted amounts. Specific Ministry of Finance approval was also required for all but the smallest outlays, even within previously approved budget totals.

The Ministry of Civil Service Affairs and Housing had to approve University organization charts and staffing plans. The University could create or eliminate positions—even secretarial or janitorial positions—only with the approval of the Ministry. The Ministry, however, could—and did—add or eliminate positions at the University on its own initiative. University faculty and staff were officially civil servants, subject to the employment conditions and compensation schedules established by the Ministry of Civil Service Affairs and Housing. University administrators had little flexibility in personnel matters, and this flexibility was achieved only through direct intervention by high-level University officials with the Ministry.

Enrollment

At the beginning of the reform effort in 2003, the University enrolled a total of about 8,600 students, about three-quarters of whom were women.[9] (See Figure 1.1.) The University provided separate campuses for

---

[9]   In Qatar, women have traditionally stayed close to their families and attended university locally, while more men have either chosen to study abroad or not to attend university. According to Qatar's 2004 census data, women age 25–29 are almost twice as likely to have

Figure 1.1
Gender and Nationality of Qatar University Students in 2003

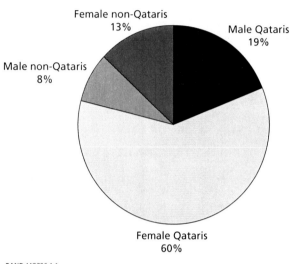

Female non-Qataris
13%

Male Qataris
19%

Male non-Qataris
8%

Female Qataris
60%

RAND *MG796-1.1*

men and for women, and all classes and extracurricular activities were gender-segregated. The same mixed-gender faculty, however, taught both men and women. This separation of men and women undergraduate students was not altered by the reform and remains today.

Qatari nationals who qualify for admission attend QU free of charge. Non-Qataris may enroll in the University, but typically must pay tuition.[10] About one-fifth of the students enrolled in QU in 2003 were non-Qataris.

Academic Programs

Each college of the University awarded bachelor's degrees in its areas of specialization. In addition, the University awarded two different postgraduate degrees in 2003: a one-year diploma in Education and a

---

pursued post-secondary education than men in the same age group (Planning Council, Government of Qatar, 2004). These factors may account for the imbalance in gender distribution at QU.

[10]   QU offers scholarships for some non-Qataris.

Master of Business Administration. However, enrollment in graduate programs was extremely small—less than 1 percent of students enrolled at QU in 2003 were registered in these programs. The language of instruction in three of the University's colleges—Engineering, Science, and Business and Economics—was English. The remaining three colleges taught in Arabic.

Before the reform effort, the University operated a Foundation Program for students accepted into the College of Science or the College of Engineering, with the aim of improving incoming students' skills in English, mathematics, and computer science to the levels necessary for university courses in science and engineering.

The University also operated a so-called Parallel Program in the afternoons and evenings, after regular University class hours. Admissions requirements for the Parallel Program were less stringent than for regular University academic programs, and the Parallel Program attracted a combination of students who had failed to meet regular admissions requirements, students whose education had been interrupted after secondary school,[11] and students whose work or family obligations precluded them from attending classes during regular University class hours. In theory, graduation requirements for the Parallel Program were the same as for the regular degree programs. (Whether this was truly the case was contentious.) Importantly, students enrolled in the Parallel Program were required to pay tuition.

Each college of the University set its own admissions standards, specifying which of two secondary school academic tracks—"science" or "literary"—would be acceptable and setting a minimum acceptable score on the appropriate examination. As a consequence, transfer from one college to another was very difficult. In effect, students were accepted by and subsequently enrolled in a particular college rather than in the larger University.

---

[11] The results of the school-leaving examination are valid for only two years. Students who did not enroll in the University within two years of secondary school graduation were consequently ineligible for regular admission to the University unless they retook the school-leaving examination.

Faculty

When the reform effort began in 2003, QU had about 400 faculty members. Forty-five percent of faculty were Qatari and the rest were expatriates. About 30 percent of the QU faculty were female. Although the University had no formal system of granting tenure, Qatari faculty members were, in effect, appointed for life. The University had no effective procedures for reviewing the performance of faculty members or for removing poorly performing Qatari faculty members.

Expatriate faculty members were almost always hired on one-year contracts, which might or might not be renewed from one year to the next. The process for deciding to renew or not to renew contracts was widely reported to be opaque. Since there was no formal appraisal system, personnel decisions were based on the personal judgment of the college administration in coordination with the central administration. Expatriate faculty members were paid less than Qatari faculty. Further, a survey of compensation at public universities in the Gulf region undertaken by the staff supporting the QU reform project found that both Qataris and non-Qataris earned less at QU than their counterparts at universities in Kuwait, the United Arab Emirates, or Oman. Finally, opportunities for career development—attending academic conferences or specialized courses, for example—were very limited for expatriate faculty.

Research

Before the reform, the University operated five research centers established to conduct applied research.[12] These centers were intended to make the expertise of University faculty available for the benefit of the larger Qatari society, and some research activities in the centers were supported by contracts with local industry. The five centers were physically separate from the University's main campus. Although each center specialized in particular subjects and was staffed by faculty from particular University colleges, none had a formal affiliation with any

---

[12] The centers were the Scientific Applied Research Center, the Sira and Sunna Research Center, the Educational Research Center, the Documentation and Humanities Research Center, and the National Center for Economic Research.

of the University colleges. Neither was there any effective coordination of academic and research activity. Each center had its own director, administrative staff, and budget.

The Need for Reform

In its earlier years, Qatar University had been regarded by many observers—both inside and outside Qatar—as one of the better universities in the Middle East. By a number of measures, however, the University's performance had been deteriorating for several years before the reforms were launched.

Some of these shortcomings were documented in admirably candid internal studies undertaken by the University itself (University Evaluation Committee, 2002; Academic Committee, 2000). Additional indicators of recent University performance were gathered directly from University records by RQPI and QU staff during the first year of the reform effort. The average time required for students to complete degree programs was lengthening (see Figures 1.2 and 1.3), and a growing fraction of the students who did graduate did so with very poor grades.[13]

For the ten years before the reforms began, the size of the faculty remained roughly constant, while the number of students grew rapidly. Consequently, the number of students per faculty member was also rising—from a ratio of 16:1 in 1993 to 20:1 in 2003.

Qualitative indicators of student engagement also suggested problems—particularly among male students. Male students, for example, were seldom seen on campus outside of class hours. Visiting advisors to QU in the fall of 2003 were struck by the contrast between a lively women's campus and a largely deserted men's campus at noon on a regular class day. Anecdotal reports abounded of poor student class attendance, lackadaisical approaches to studies, and occasional

---

[13] For years, a cumulative grade point average (GPA) of 1.5 (on a 4-point scale) was sufficient for graduation. At the beginning of the 2003–2004 academic year, the standard for graduation was raised to 2.0.

Figure 1.2
Qatar University Student Time to Graduation, 1998–2003

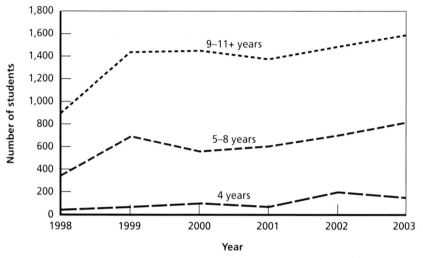

RAND *MG796-1.2*

Figure 1.3
1998–1999 Cohort Graduation Rate, by Number of Years to Graduation

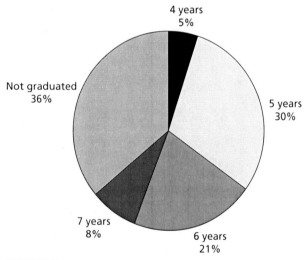

RAND *MG796-1.3*

hectoring of faculty by students or parents about grades. Few extra-curricular activities were available to students. At the beginning of the reform effort, students, faculty, and administrators agreed that no University community existed in any meaningful sense.

By some objective measures, the quality of the faculty was also declining. Internal studies documented, for example that the faculty was becoming more junior. Within a faculty of roughly constant size, the number of lecturers (as opposed to assistant professors and professors) was rising, and the number of full professors had fallen sharply in the years before the reform (see Figure 1.4). The number of research papers published by QU faculty had fallen significantly. Faculty seminars, which had once been frequent, had decreased significantly in quality and quantity by 2003.

More-qualitative measures also suggested problems with the faculty. Morale was widely reported to be low. Faculty were seldom found on campus when they were not teaching. Indeed, the previous President had tried unsuccessfully to enforce a formal requirement that faculty spend a minimum number of hours on campus each week. Respected

Figure 1.4
Number of Full, Associate, and Assistant Professors, 1994–2003

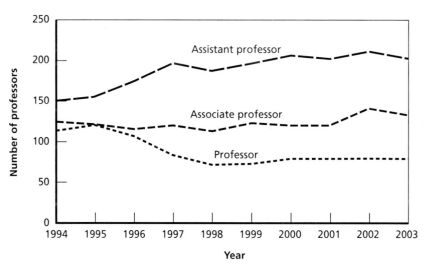

faculty were departing for better-paying positions in state-owned and private companies. In earlier years, some of the colleges in the University had regularly convened advisory panels of respected academics to review college programs and research. This practice had been largely abandoned several years before the reforms began, however.

In the years leading up to the reform effort, the University's internal administration had become increasingly centralized, with more and more decisions passing through offices of the President, the Vice President for Academic Affairs, and the Vice President for Finance and Administration. Faculty complained that the central administration was usurping authorities that had traditionally rested with the faculty and with academic departments: faculty recruiting, retention, and promotion; curriculum development; and maintenance of academic standards. (In the period immediately before the reform, for example, final decisions about faculty hiring and retention were made by the University's Vice President for Academic Affairs, not by academic departments or colleges. The Vice President even decided which curricula vitae the departments and colleges could review and comment on.) For their part, senior members of the previous administration responded that they had no choice but to take charge because the academic units were unable or unwilling to manage these affairs. Whatever the reasons for or the merits of administrative centralization, the predictable consequences of this shift in administrative responsibility were a "hollowing out" of colleges and academic departments and growing estrangement between the central administration and the faculty.

In 2003, the University had no written compilation of procedures documenting how important academic or administrative processes were to be conducted. Key aspects of University life were handled through sometimes inconsistent improvisation or governed by long-standing but unwritten tradition.

Lacking control over its own personnel policies, the University was unable to resist a tendency on the part of the Ministry of Civil Service Affairs and Housing to create positions for ever larger numbers of civil servants within the University. Many of these appointments were understood as sinecures. The appointees were not involved in the life of the University and were rarely seen on campus. The University was widely regarded as overstaffed administratively even in 1993, when it had two administrators for each faculty member. By 2003, the ratio had grown to three to one.

The University was also facing financial difficulties. In the decade before the reforms began, University funding had not kept pace with rising numbers of students. In the mid- to late 1990s, government allocations for most purposes—not just for the University—were severely constrained because oil prices were weak and because the government was investing heavily in developing offshore gas fields. But even as resources became more plentiful in the new century, allocations to the University remained constrained; some observers suggested this was a reflection that the higher authorities lacked confidence in the University to utilize additional resources effectively.

Finally and most importantly, evidence was accumulating by 2003 that the University was failing to meet the needs of the larger Qatari society. Employers in Qatar—in both the public and private sectors—reported that few University graduates met required standards for employment. Such views were common before the reform began, and members of the University reform team subsequently verified these views through interviews with local employers and members of the University community in late 2003 and early 2004. Indeed, so bad had the situation become that QU graduates who lacked skills matched to the needs of the Qatari economy routinely enrolled in training programs managed by the Ministry of Civil Service Affairs and Housing.

By the summer of 2003, reforms of some key elements of Qatar's educational system were well under way. These actions in other parts of the Qatari educational system served to make the absence of reform in the national university increasingly conspicuous—especially since both objective and perceptual indicators of Qatar University performance had been deteriorating for several years. It was against this backdrop that a major overhaul of Qatar University was launched in the fall of 2003.

CHAPTER TWO

Designing the Reform Agenda

Senior members of Qatar University—including the soon-to-be President—had already been discussing the broad nature of necessary reforms for several months before the new leadership team took over in August 2003. Members of the RQPI staff had participated in some of these discussions, and a consensus had gradually emerged regarding a process by which the University might arrive at a concrete and actionable agenda for reform. This chapter describes the role of the University in leading the reform and how RQPI and QU organized the effort. It also describes the objectives of the reform and obstacles the University faced in meeting those objectives. Finally, we present the reform agenda that was accepted by the Emir and launched in 2004.

The fundamental principle of the reform effort was that QU itself had to initiate and lead the reform. All parties agreed from the outset that leading University personnel had to play the central role first in articulating and then in implementing a strategy for reform. Equally important, all recommendations relating to reform of the University had first to be accepted by the University's leadership and then forwarded to the Emir, in his capacity as Supreme Head of the University, for approval. Approved reform proposals would then be implemented by University staff acting on the authority delegated to the University by the Emir.

There were three reasons for insisting that the University itself should be the primary agent of reform. First, University faculty and staff knew better than any outsider the University's strengths and weaknesses, the challenges and the opportunities it faced, and the educational needs of the larger Qatari society. Outside analysts and experts might suggest alternative approaches and provide examples of how successful universities elsewhere deal with issues similar to those faced by QU, but only the faculty and staff of QU could understand fully how experience elsewhere could or should be modified to fit QU's circumstances.

Second, the success of the reform depended critically on a willingness on the part of most (but not necessarily all) of the University's faculty and staff to accept "ownership" of both the reform process and the specific elements of the reform agenda. All parties to the reform effort agreed that successful universities operate best when faculty and staff (and, for some purposes, students) share a common vision of the university's mission and the strategies chosen to fulfill that mission.

Finally, a key objective of the reform effort was to create within the University a capability for continuing self-assessment and adjustment. The best way to build this capacity, all parties agreed, was to engage key members of the University community in the reform process from the very beginning.

Although University personnel were to be the primary actors in the reform process, there was a consensus that outsiders could and should make important contributions. Leaders and administrators from other universities could share their experiences and observation with the QU leadership, identifying policies and practices that had been successful elsewhere and warning of pitfalls encountered in other university reform efforts. Outside analysts would work side by side with members of the QU faculty and staff to structure deliberations about reform strategies and to assemble the evidentiary base for specific reform proposals. Perhaps most importantly, outside experts and analysts could approach QU's reform in a more impartial fashion than could members of the QU faculty and staff. Although outsiders might occasionally be disadvantaged by not understanding the full history of how particular polices, practices, or institutional arrangements at QU had come into being, these outsiders might make significant contributions by posing difficult questions, which in turn might force QU personnel to reconsider the appropriateness or the effectiveness of current practices.

A principal challenge in designing the reform process was to create mechanisms that would facilitate close collaboration and trusted, constructive debate among QU personnel and outside experts and analysts.

Organizing for Reform

QU and RQPI agreed that inspiration for and leadership of the reform effort should emerge from a high-level **Senior Reform Committee (SRC)** made up of senior members of the University and a few highly experienced outside experts.[1] The SRC was jointly chaired by the President of the University and the leader of the RQPI project team. The QU President appointed five additional members of the Committee from among the University's faculty and administrators. As the SRC was originally constituted, these University members of the Committee included the Chief Academic Officer, the Chief Administrative and Financial Officer, the Dean of Student Affairs, and two prominent faculty members.

The QU members were joined on the SRC by five experts on higher education from leading universities in the United States.[2] In the original constitution of the SRC, these visiting experts included a former president, a former provost, a serving provost, a former chief financial officer, and a distinguished professor of higher education. These outside members of the SRC were recruited by RQPI and approved for their roles by the QU President.

The SRC was not a decisionmaking body. Rather, it served as a forum for candid discussion about the mission of the University, the obstacles the University faced in trying to fulfill this mission, possible strategies for overcoming these obstacles, and practical steps toward

---

[1] See Appendix A for a complete list of SRC members that served during the three-year reform project.

[2] In its original composition, the SRC's non-QU members were all from U.S. universities. During the implementation phases of the reform, a professor from a major British university joined the Committee.

implementing reforms. These discussions helped to shape decisions by the President regarding specific reform proposals to be forwarded to the Emir. This organizational structure is shown in Figure 2.1. In its discussions, the SRC sought to arrive at consensus on key points but felt no absolute requirement to do so. Final decisions on reform proposals were made by the President with the benefit of guidance from the Committee. As a practical matter, the SRC did reach consensus on virtually all important matters. As a member of the SRC, the President was a party to this consensus, and consequently the proposals submitted to the Emir reflected both the decisions of the President and the shared views of the SRC.

The SRC met four times from January through June 2004, for two days of discussion at each meeting. Some of the visiting members of the SRC arrived in Doha a few days before meetings to engage relevant QU staff on subjects of particular interest.

The SRC's meeting time was quite limited and therefore valuable. In order to make this time as productive as possible, the University and RQPI assembled a small **reform project staff** of about a dozen people (the number varied slightly from one SRC meeting to the next) to serve as a secretariat for the SRC. The staff was made up of RQPI analysts and QU faculty members appointed by the President. The President

Figure 2.1
Organization of Reform Project in Year 1

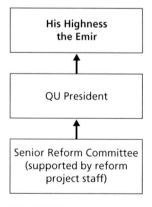

appointed a mix of senior faculty with in-depth knowledge of QU and its history and promising younger faculty whom the President hoped might grow into the future leaders of QU.[3]

This reform project staff had two principal responsibilities. The first was to prepare for each SRC meeting by establishing an agenda for discussion and collecting relevant background information. The staff conducted interviews inside and outside the University, gathered data from University recordkeeping systems and from previous internal studies, and sought information about policies and practices at other universities—all as necessary to inform discussions planned for each SRC meeting. In effect, the staff served as the eyes and ears of the Committee. For each SRC meeting, the staff produced a detailed read-ahead memorandum for SRC members, which framed the issues to be discussed and summarized the staff's findings relevant to these issues.

The second responsibility of the staff was to produce an analytic summary of the discussions at each SRC meeting, capturing the main points of the Committee's deliberations, the Committee's principal recommendations, and—most important—the specific arguments advanced in support of these recommendations.

Both the read-ahead memorandums and the after-meeting summaries were fully joint efforts. Typically, RQPI staff members took the lead in drafting these documents, but both types of documents were reviewed carefully and revised extensively in consultation with the QU members of the reform project staff.

In order to allow candid and constructive discussion, the meetings of the SRC were not open to the general University community or to the public at large. Written summaries of the meetings avoided attributing particular views to individual Committee members.

The members of the reform project staff attended all SRC meetings. They were, of course, available to clarify points of background, but they were also encouraged to take an active role in SRC discussions, adding their operational-level perspective to the strategic deliberations

---

[3] In subsequent years, as attention shifted from developing to implementing a reform strategy, the President appointed different junior faculty members to the reform project staff in order to broaden the group of faculty with direct experience of the reform effort.

of the SRC itself. Members of the staff were asked to hold confidential the deliberations of the SRC until the President was ready to announce specific reforms to the general University community.

Objectives and Obstacles

The SRC began its deliberations with a concerted effort to articulate the principal objectives of the reform. What did they want QU to become? They also sought to identify the specific obstacles that would have to be overcome if their vision for the University were to become a reality.

The Role of Qatar University in Qatari Society

The first major topic addressed by the SRC was the appropriate role of QU in Qatari society. The SRC affirmed QU's status as the primary option for qualified Qatari students seeking post-secondary education. QU should also serve, the SRC recommended, as the principal reservoir of knowledge and expertise for the rapidly developing State of Qatar. The SRC proposed that QU should contribute to the nation's broad social development by setting intellectual standards. For example, the University's own standards for admission would become *de facto* standards for required secondary school achievement. According to the SRC, the University should also be instrumental in recognizing intellectual expertise and achievement, by promoting respectful and fact-based discussion and debate of key issues facing the country, and by promoting public and governmental understanding of these issues.

Within its articulation of the University's broad role, the SRC offered specific recommendations that would define the academic character of the University. The SRC agreed that QU should serve students who are qualified and motivated to pursue rigorous *academic* education at the post-secondary level. QU should aim to serve principally average and above-average students and should develop strategies to give diligent students every possible opportunity for academic success. But, the SRC stressed, QU could not and should not try to be all things to all students. It is not a vocational school, for example. And although QU should offer foundation programs to strengthen the preparation of diligent students, the University should be under no obligation or expectation to serve students who are not qualified for serious university-level studies. Other institutions in the country should pursue the worthwhile goals of providing post-secondary training to students who are not prepared for or who do not want rigorous academic education.

The SRC also addressed, in broad terms, what the University should teach. Through extensive interviews, the reform project staff had documented widespread support within Qatari society for a broadened university education that would prepare graduates for success in a demanding and unpredictably changing world. QU graduates, the SRC agreed, should possess a set of core skills—beyond expertise in a chosen field of specialization—that would equip them for successful professional life in an increasingly open and competitive economy and for citizenship in Qatar's emerging democracy. In particular, students should be equipped to pursue lifelong learning and to remain independent and critical thinkers. The Committee stressed the University's obligation to instill in students an understanding of and appreciation for their national identity and to acquaint them with foreign cultures, practices, and views and to encourage students to approach foreign cultures with open minds, respect, and tolerance.

Although the views of Qatar's governmental, commercial, and social leaders are important in shaping QU's curriculum, the SRC insisted that the University and its faculty must *lead* such thinking, by anticipating needs for an educated population that may not yet be apparent to others in the society. Finally, the SRC urged that QU should remain primarily an undergraduate institution. There was general recognition that this decision could be revisited in the future in response to changing needs, but there was a strong sentiment on the part of the SRC that Qatari students might be better served by going abroad for postgraduate studies. They argued that these students will benefit from exposure to foreign cultures and intellectual environments in the course of their studies.

The SRC discussed at length the place of research at QU, noting the difficulty of maintaining a strong program of research in a primarily undergraduate institution. Ultimately, the SRC came to emphasize the importance of a broader concept—"scholarly endeavor," within which they included traditional university research, other kinds of rigorous inquiry, and pedagogical innovation. The primary mission of QU, the SRC noted, should be teaching, but scholarly endeavor is essential to teaching and learning at a University level. All faculty, the Committee recommended, should be expected to engage in scholarly endeavors. Moreover, active participation in such endeavors should be a part of every undergraduate's experience at QU.[4]

Obstacles to Be Overcome

Having outlined the basic mission of the University, the SRC sought to identify the principal obstacles to the University's fulfilling this mission. The fact-finding efforts of the reform project staff, which included both documentary research and interviews with University faculty and students, had brought to the Committee's attention many specific difficulties facing the University at the time the reform effort began. The SRC grouped these multiple difficulties into seven major problems that would have to be resolved in the reform effort:

1. The University was unable to manage its own affairs. The University had never achieved autonomy from the Ministry of Civil Service Affairs and Housing (in personnel matters) or the Ministry of Finance (in budgetary matters). This contributed to the University lacking the basic administrative infrastructure to exercise autonomy—if and when it were granted.
2. The administration of the University was overly centralized, with the offices of the President, the Chief Academic Officer, and the Chief Financial and Administrative Officer performing academic and administrative functions more properly delegated to colleges and academic departments.
3. Academic and administrative structures had not kept pace with changing demands on the University or with international trends in higher education. The internal organization of the

---

[4] When the reform project began in 2004, there were few opportunities for undergraduate involvement in research in Qatar. Since then, Qatar Foundation introduced the Undergraduate Research Experience Program (UREP), aimed at significantly expanding support for undergraduate research and scholarly endeavors for university students in the country.

University was inadequate to support the mission that the SRC had envisioned.

4. The University had no systematic academic planning—no regular or routine approach to considering what should be taught, how, and by whom.

5. The University's academic structure was one of largely isolated colleges with little common activity or the mutual reinforcement that would make the University more than simply the sum of its various parts.

6. Faculty quality and performance were inadequate for a university of the stature that QU aspired to achieve.

7. Faculty exhibited little "ownership" of or commitment to the mission of the University. In too many cases, faculty simply taught their assigned classes but contributed little to the broader life of the University community.

The Reform Agenda

The principal product of the SRC's deliberations during the first year of the reform effort was a set of specific, actionable proposals for reform of the University that were forwarded to His Highness the Emir for approval. In June 2004, shortly after the final SRC meeting of the first year, the two co-chairpersons of the SRC—the University President and the RQPI project leader—presented to the Emir an outline of a new view of QU's mission[5] along with specific proposals for accomplishing this mission and an estimate of the financial resources that would be required to implement the proposed reforms.

The principal recommendations for reform were these:

Recommendation 1: Establish university autonomy. The SRC recommended that the Emir delegate his authority as Supreme Head of the University to a Board of Regents composed of prominent Qataris drawn from the local governmental and business communities and

---

[5]   During the implementation phase of the reform, the University ratified a formal statement of the revised QU mission.

international experts on higher education. The Emir would appoint the Regents, and they in turn would exercise external oversight over the University, with power to appoint or to remove the University President and to review and approve University policies, bylaws, and proposed major structural or programmatic changes. The Regents would review and approve the University's annual budget request to the Ministry of Finance and review significant reallocations of resources within the context of an overall budget. The Regents would also monitor the University's performance and service to the nation and recommend appropriate changes whenever either might be unsatisfactory. Further, the SRC recommended that the University be released from oversight by the Ministry of Civil Service Affairs and Housing and empowered to establish its own personnel policies and compensation schedules. Similarly, once the University's annual budget is approved by the Ministry of Finance, the University should have full power to allocate that budget as it sees fit. The SRC recognized that a significant strengthening of the University's personnel and financial management systems would be required for it to exercise true autonomy in these areas.

Recommendation 2: Decentralize administrative arrangements. The SRC recommended that responsibility for academic decisions—faculty appointments, promotions, course design, etc.—and routine financial management be returned to colleges and academic departments. Colleges and departments would have to be strengthened and their personnel trained to assume these newly delegated responsibilities. The role of central administrative offices should be to train and to support staffs in subsidiary academic units and to ensure that policies and practices are broadly consistent across the University. The SRC also recommended creating within the central administration an Office of Institutional Research and Planning to coordinate the overall reform process and facilitate university-wide academic and strategic planning.[6] The administrative and financial structure of the University—at the

---

[6]   The name of this office was subsequently changed to the Office of Institutional Planning and Development, and its Director was named a Vice President. In addition, titles of the Associate Vice Presidents for Student Affairs and for Research were changed to Vice President. Throughout the remainder of this monograph, we employ current titles in use at QU.

central, college, and departmental levels—should be strengthened to allow the University to reclaim its administrative autonomy from government ministries. A manual of policies and procedures and related faculty and student handbooks should be developed, disseminated, and adhered to. Finally, according to the SRC, an Academic Senate, elected by the faculty, should be established to *advise* the central administration on University-level academic decisions and policies.

Recommendation 3: Modify the academic structure of the University. The SRC recommended that the existing Colleges of Humanities and Science be combined into a College of Arts and Sciences. Around the College of Arts and Sciences and drawing on its resources as appropriate would be five additional colleges for specialized or professional study: Engineering, Business, Law, Education, and Sharia. The SRC recommended merging the regular degree programs of the University and the Parallel Program and establishing common admissions standards for all University students. Also, the SRC recommended integrating research and academic activities by merging the existing independent research centers into the appropriate colleges.

Recommendation 4: Institute a core curriculum. The SRC recommended that the University establish a core curriculum to be completed by all graduating students. Beyond the substantive knowledge required for success in a particular field of study, this core curriculum would provide QU students with a true liberal education, the foundation for academic achievement, professional success, good citizenship, and a rewarding life of the mind. The core curriculum would communicate a sense for and knowledge of history, culture, literature, government, and science. It would also promote and exercise essential skills such as critical thinking and effective communication. The core curriculum should be flexibly structured, recognizing and allowing multiple approaches to acquiring a set of skills and knowledge common to all QU graduates. The SRC recommended that all parts of the University should contribute to designing and teaching the core curriculum, with the new College of Arts and Sciences exercising primary responsibility for coordinating the efforts of other colleges.

Recommendation 5: Introduce University-wide academic planning. The SRC recommended that University-wide academic planning be instituted. Colleges and academic departments would bear primary responsibility for assessing and forecasting society's needs for higher education, evaluating their own academic programs, and offering plans to close any gaps revealed through these analyses. The central administration would provide administrative support for this academic planning by colleges and departments. The central administration would also review and approve plans for significant changes in academic programs. Finally, the SRC pointed out that academic planning can be effective only when closely linked to financial and personnel planning.

Recommendation 6: Improve management of faculty and staff. The SRC offered a suite of recommendations aimed at improving the quality and the performance of QU faculty and staff. They proposed increased compensation for both faculty and staff, but insisted that pay be linked to performance through a program of regular performance evaluations. They further recommended that the President of the University should enjoy some flexibility in setting compensation to respond to changing market conditions and to recognize special contributions by individual faculty or staff. Tenure or some other form of job security should be offered to high-performing faculty, and procedures should be established for releasing redundant or poorly performing faculty and staff. All faculty and staff should have opportunities for professional development through courses, training programs, conference attendance, sabbatical leave, and the like. The duration of contracts for expatriate faculty should be lengthened, and distinctions between Qatari and expatriate faculty reduced. The University should undertake to identify and to transmit to faculty the best pedagogical practices found within the University and in universities elsewhere. Finally, according to the SRC recommendations, the President should have authorization and budget resources to hire up to 20 new "lead scholars" of established reputation to strengthen the faculty.

Recommendation 7: Foster and support student achievement. The SRC recommended that the University set a single minimum admission standard, doing away with the previous lower admission standard applied to students in the Parallel Program. The SRC accepted, however, that higher supplemental standards might be set for admissions to particular specialized programs of study. Ideally, the University would also work to base its admissions decisions on more and better evidence of academic potential than the current single school-leaving examination. The Committee recommended that the preparatory Foundation Program be expanded and made available to students entering all programs within the University. The SRC recommended expanded and strengthened orientation programs for new students and academic counseling for all students. Academic regulations should be clarified and uniformly enforced. Finally, the Committee recommended creation of an honors college or programs for students who perform particularly well. The benefits of admission to the honors college or programs would include access to advanced courses, opportunities for foreign study, and assistance in finding employment or entering appropriate postgraduate study upon graduation.

Supplementary recommendation: Explore limited moves toward coeducation. The SRC recognized the cultural importance of gender-segregated education in Qatar and did not recommend changing the existing division of QU into men's and women's campuses. The external members of the SRC did, however, suggest that additional and *voluntary* extracurricular activities and opportunities be offered in coeducational settings. Arguing that skilled professionals will increasingly be required to function in gender-mixed environments, the SRC recommended that new postgraduate programs established at QU be coeducational.[7]

Launching the Reforms

In presenting these recommendations to the Emir, the co-chairpersons of the SRC proposed that reform should begin immediately, with the proposed changes in academic structure to be effective in the next aca-

---

[7]   Due to the sensitive nature of this recommendation and the significant changes that would be required in the University's policies and procedures to introduce coeducation successfully, the University leadership decided this was not a matter to be addressed during the reform implementation process. For this reason, this recommendation is not addressed again in this monograph.

demic year—about three months after the presentation to the Emir. They also proposed that work should begin immediately on a number of high-priority items of the reform agenda. To coordinate reform-related activities, the University proposed to give this responsibility to the Office of Institutional Planning and Development (OIPD). When the major tasks of the reform had been completed in a few years' time, this office would assume responsibility for continuing evaluation and adjustment of University structures, programs, and policies.

The co-chairpersons of the SRC requested that His Highness the Emir approve the reform agenda as presented. In addition, they requested that he exercise his direct authority one final time as Supreme Head of the University to launch the reform. Specifically, they requested the Emir

- To approve the proposed changes in academic and administrative structures
- To approve a new compensation structure for University faculty and staff
- To authorize the immediate hiring of distinguished lead scholars to bolster the faculty and a number of expert advisors to assist temporarily in certain technical aspects of the reform
- To authorize the University to eliminate redundant personnel
- To issue a decree establishing the University's autonomy and instructing the Ministry of Civil Service Affairs and Housing and the Ministry of Finance to facilitate the transfer of administrative responsibility to the University
- To issue a decree establishing a Board of Regents for the University and delegating to the Regents authority to exercise oversight over the University
- To approve a supplementary budget to begin implementation of the reforms.

The Emir agreed to these requests in June 2004, and implementation of the reforms began immediately. The next chapter of this monograph describes the process of implementation.

CHAPTER THREE

Implementing the Reform Agenda

The reform implementation effort began at the end of June 2004, when His Highness the Emir accepted the new statement of QU's mission and approved the key recommendations from the SRC. The formal implementation project ended in January 2007, but the reform process itself is ongoing.

In the intervening years, the SRC and supporting staff members, other QU faculty, and selected external consultants continued to work together in the ways described in the previous chapter. Although the SRC convened less frequently,[1] significant tasks were carried out between meetings by designated reform project staff and consultants. Results of these tasks were reported back to the Committee for discussion, evaluation, and action.

While the principal recommendations described in Chapter Two guided the overall reform effort, the SRC also made numerous more detailed recommendations to support these major objectives. The planning year of the reform project provided a clear deadline, but the major challenge for the SRC and its staff lay in how to parse and sequence the activities required to realize the ambitious reform agenda. Several recommendations, while independent in principle, were interdependent in practice. For example, establishing a core curriculum could not be accomplished without academic restructuring on the one hand and academic planning on the other. Similarly, decentralizing particular administrative arrangements depended on achieving university auton-

---

[1]   The SRC met twice during each of the two full academic years of the implementation project, with a final closing session in 2007.

omy more generally. Further, as implementation got under way, the SRC and reform project staff identified a number of additional reform actions needed to support the overall recommendations. Finally, not all the reform initiatives could be undertaken concurrently. So the first critical implementation decisions concerned organizing the reform process into conceptually distinct parts and managing the order and pace of change.

The SRC recommended—and QU leadership subsequently decided—to begin the implementation process by building the institutional structures and setting out the major policies and procedures that underpinned subsequent reform initiatives. Next, the QU leadership, as advised by the SRC, sought to introduce into the day-to-day life of the University practices that would establish a culture of quality and accountability. Finally, the reformers aimed to institutionalize the changes in a revitalized and sustainable University community through actions that required its members to internalize and build on the new mission for QU. The SRC emphasized the responsibility of all members of the University community to contribute to their common intellectual life, regenerating a spirit of collegial engagement.

These stages of activity proceeded at different paces in different areas of endeavor and typically overlapped in time. In this chapter, we describe the accomplishments of the reform, organized into six domains of effort undertaken by the SRC and the staff, along with the key actions the University defined for each. For this purpose we rely on tables drawn from more detailed materials prepared in advance of the final SRC meeting. These materials were used by the SRC and its staff to evaluate the progress of the reform over the course of the implementation project's two-and-a-half-year lifespan. In each table, benchmarks are shaded to indicate the extent of their realization by the end of the implementation project.[2] The six domains are as follows: create institutional autonomy; improve University decisionmaking processes; revitalize academic offerings; improve management of faculty;

---

[2]   Throughout the implementation process, the reform project staff developed much more detailed timelines concerning the actions required to accomplish the major reform initiatives. In this chapter, we present only high-level progress benchmarks.

foster and support student achievement; and strengthen the University community.

Create Institutional Autonomy

As explained in Chapter One, QU, in its three-decade history, had never functioned as an autonomous academic institution. For purposes of academic governance, QU's President reported directly to the Emir. The University's financial matters were in the hands of the Ministry of Finance, while personnel policies and salary schedules were overseen by the Ministry of Civil Service Affairs and Housing.

The first steps toward autonomy in governance, finance, and personnel matters were taken quite rapidly, following the Emir's decision to grant autonomy to the University in the Emiri Decree (Emiri Decree, 2004). Table 3.1 shows the three types of autonomy recommended for the University, along with associated major benchmarks for each type.

Following the Emir's decree, formal autonomy in academic governance was quickly realized with the appointment of a Board of Regents and the adoption of a set of bylaws outlining the scope and limits of the Board's authority. The bylaws were drafted by the SRC, with staff assistance, after comparable instruments from modern Western universities had been collected and reviewed. A functioning Board was in place by November 2004.

Realizing autonomy in personnel self-management took longer. The civil service model that the University previously employed for hiring, retention, promotion, and termination was not appropriate for an academic institution. Additionally, titles of positions, job levels, and salary scales did not accurately reflect responsibilities, competencies, and workloads. Reform project staff compiled salary and compensation data from other universities in the region, and also gathered examples of personnel policies and procedures from Western universities to provide benchmarks for the development of a new system tailored for QU.

A key incentive was to make sufficient progress to allow faculty recruitment for open positions in the 2005–2006 academic year under improved personnel policies and procedures. Existing faculty, in con-

Table 3.1
Create Institutional Autonomy

Key Actions	Status as of January 2007
Academic Self-Governance	
Create and vest ultimate authority in a Board of Regents.	■
Appoint Board and conduct semiannual meetings.	■
Adopt bylaws for QU governance.	■
Personnel Self-Management	
Separate personnel management from Ministry of Civil Service Affairs and Housing.	■
Develop/implement new hiring/firing/retention policies and procedures.	■
Develop/implement new salary and compensation schedules.	■
Financial Self-Governance	
Separate financial governance from the Ministry of Finance.	■
Develop/implement a financial accounting system (ORACLE).	■
Develop/implement new budget system (functional- versus account-driven).	▦

■ Achieved   ▦ Partially achieved   ☐ In progress

trast, continued under their former contracts. As a result, they felt disadvantaged relative to new faculty, a situation that did not begin to be remedied until the 2006–2007 academic year.

As Table 3.1 suggests, implementing financial autonomy was even more complex and was not completely achieved by the end of the implementation project. The SRC and the staff had to start with an overall budget approved by the Ministry of Finance for QU; it was organized by major budget categories or "chapters" (e.g., personnel, equipment and supplies) but not further disaggregated by colleges or departments. Financial records were on paper, rather than in a modern, computerized system. Complicating this transition further, Qatar's fiscal year runs from April 1 through March 31. Therefore, a draft QU budget would have to be in place in February 2005 for approval by the Ministry of Finance before the start of the next fiscal year.

The SRC and the staff concluded that it was not possible to establish a financial accounting system in time to prepare a budget proposal for the upcoming fiscal year. They considered two options for resolving this issue:

1. Continue the existing arrangements for another year, delaying QU's assumption of financial self-governance until the fiscal year beginning in April 2006.
2. Take on financial autonomy immediately, with University departments, colleges, and other offices taking responsibility for their own budgets but relying on the Ministry of Finance's accounting system until QU's own system was operational.

The University leadership chose the second option so that QU unit heads could begin the practice of autonomous financial decisionmaking. By the following year, the University installed financial accounting software and had a base budget in place from which to project future expenses.

However, as Table 3.1 suggests, the transition to financial autonomy was regarded as not yet complete by the end of the implementation project. Annual budgets for most budgetary units were still being prepared on the basis of prior expenditure categories rather than on academic plans and priorities. For instance, budgeting rarely reflected a forward-looking assessment of emerging needs to develop new programs or courses or to acquire new types of pedagogical materials demanded by a core curriculum then being organized around inquiry-based learning. Instead, fiscal proposals still tended to reflect a backward look at what had been spent previously in established budget categories and an estimate of what would be needed to undertake the same sorts of activities, allowing for expected increases in numbers of students and/ or costs of personnel and acquisitions. Given these practices, the SRC reemphasized its recommendation that the University transition away from old budgeting practices toward more functionally oriented budgeting. The transition to functional budgeting would entail further revisions to the financial accounting system; it would also require more experience with effective budgeting practices and with linking functional budget decisions to longer-term program priorities. All of this would take additional time to implement.

Improve University Decisionmaking Processes

The SRC viewed decentralizing decisionmaking authority to appropriate levels and units in the university as a logical extension of institutional autonomy. The SRC and QU leadership embraced the principle that decisionmaking should, in all cases, be delegated to the lowest-level unit possible, consistent with the effective and efficient discharge of unit responsibilities. Such a transition entailed both structural and cultural changes, as depicted in Table 3.2.

First, the University had to establish more decentralized and differentiated structures and mechanisms for decisionmaking to accompany the University's new organizational structure. New bylaws and procedures were required to make clear where authority and account-

Table 3.2
Improve University Decisionmaking Processes

Key Actions	Status as of January 2007
Create new structures for delegation of decisionmaking.	■
Adopt academic bylaws that give responsibility for academic decisions and routine financial management to colleges and departments.	■
Create OIPD.	■
Practice evidence-based decisionmaking at all levels of the University.	▨
Develop academic and management information systems.	▨
Establish a faculty senate.	■

■ Achieved   ▨ Partially achieved   □ In progress

ability for different types of decisions would be vested. In the past, for instance, the Ministry of Civil Service Affairs and Housing had to approve all new hires. In the new environment, department chairs would nominate new faculty, and college deans would approve those appointments.

The pre-reform organizational structure of QU posed major impediments to this new form of decisionmaking. As Figure 3.1 illustrates, the pre-reform organizational structure essentially precluded decentralization, because the levels and entities below the office of the University President to which decisionmaking could be delegated systematically were not well defined. The University needed a new organizational framework to permit allocation of different authorities and associated accountabilities. Figure 3.2 shows the post-reform organizational structure.

To develop these improved structures and procedures, the SRC and QU leadership again tasked project staff with locating and reviewing relevant precedents from other universities, identifying appropri-

Figure 3.1
QU Organizational Structure Before the Reform

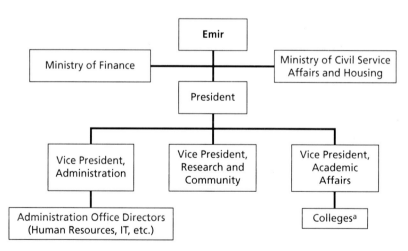

[a]Five separate colleges with no organized academic planning, no shared core curriculum, and no interdisciplinary interaction.

RAND *MG796-3.1*

Figure 3.2
QU Organizational Structure After the Reform

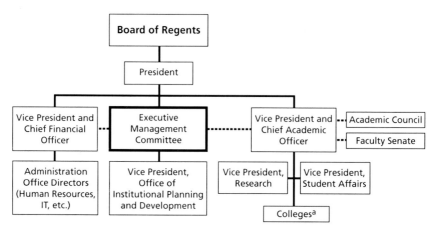

a Six separate colleges (one College of Arts and Sciences plus five specialized colleges) with common academic planning, a shared core curriculum, and plans to introduce interdisciplinary programs and major/minor combinations.

RAND *MG796-3.2*

ate options for QU, and summarizing their strengths and weaknesses. These kinds of background materials and assessments provided a rich basis for SRC deliberation about the institutional mechanisms that might best serve QU's needs, with the final choices being made by QU leadership.

Perhaps the most difficult aspect of the move to improved decisionmaking processes, however, was the cultural change it necessitated—specifically, shifting from a culture of centralized control to one of autonomy with accountability. This shift required QU leadership to place greater trust in faculty and administrators at lower levels of the University hierarchy, many of whom lacked management experience. At the same time, the latter had to exercise some leadership on their own, making and justifying decisions and taking the risk of being wrong. These prospects were discomforting to University community members on both sides of the hierarchical divide.

The election of an academic senate, late in the implementation project and unprecedented in the region, signaled a significant change to a new culture of faculty self-determination. Like many academic senates, its role is intended to be consultative and advisory rather than legislative. Nevertheless, it gives the faculty a strong and formal voice in the new institutional environment.

Revitalize Academic Structures and Services[3]

Three of the SRC's major reform recommendations centered around revitalizing and modernizing academic structures and services, ranging from how they are organized and planned to how their contents are chosen, delivered, and evaluated. Table 3.3 outlines accomplishments in this domain. The discussion that follows focuses on major academic changes.

QU leadership acted immediately on the SRC's recommendation to reorganize the academic structure of the University (see Chapter Two, Recommendation 3), creating a single College of Arts and Sciences (CAS) by joining two formerly disparate colleges (Humanities, Science) and, in the process, combining some small departments into larger ones (e.g., Mathematics and Physics). The reorganization of the CAS departments addressed the SRC's notion that QU should give priority and emphasis to practical areas of study seen to be immediately useful and relevant to Qatari society during this important phase of the country's development.

Concurrently, the University approved the development of a core curriculum, to be coordinated by the CAS. The University also decided to create a new College of Law, separating it from the College of Sharia

---

[3]   The discussion in this section focuses on the development and approval of an academic plan encompassing all colleges and departments, because it integrates most of the elements subsumed by the academic revitalization goal. For instance, this activity began by taking into account large-scale collegiate restructuring (including the elimination of the Parallel Program and integration of research efforts into the resulting academic units) and extended to the design of core curriculum elements distributed among the units as well regular academic program reviews and updates into future plans. An information technology (IT) infrastructure adequate to enable tracking of enrollments in classes and progress toward majors as well as to permit posting of updated course descriptions, syllabi, and other curricular materials was largely in place by the end of the implementation period.

Table 3.3
Revitalize Academic Structures and Services

Key Actions	Status as of January 2007
Create a College of Arts and Sciences.	Achieved
Merge independent research centers into colleges and create Office of Research.	Achieved
Eliminate the Parallel Program.	In progress
Develop and obtain approval for University-wide academic plan.	Achieved
Improve IT infrastructure and services.	Achieved
Develop and introduce a core curriculum.	Partially achieved
Integrate department/program reviews into planning processes.	In progress

■ Achieved   ▦ Partially achieved   ☐ In progress

and Islamic Studies. The Colleges of Engineering, Education, and Business also made changes in their departmental structures. The new structures were in place when faculty, staff, and students returned from the summer break at the start of the 2004–2005 academic year.

Not surprisingly, the changed academic arrangements in the new College of Arts and Sciences received mixed reactions: a sizable proportion of the faculty viewed them with skepticism, while some faculty members expressed strong opposition. Still others believed that restructuring decisions should have been made after, not before, the recommended University-wide academic planning effort (see Chapter Two, Recommendation 5).

Although the decision to create the CAS and merge departments was largely unilateral, the QU leadership strongly believed in the importance of engaging members of the University in a decentralized University-wide academic planning process that was initiated in 2005–2006 academic year.[4] Accordingly, in winter 2005, the SRC requested

---

[4]   See Appendix D for more detail on the academic planning initiative.

that RQPI staff conduct focus groups with representatives of all colleges and departments in the new academic structure. The objective was to gather input from the University community about the chief aims that should guide the academic planning processes. About 15 percent of the faculty were recruited for this exercise, proportionately distributed over academic units. The groups were reminded of QU's mission (to be "a model national university that offers a high quality, learning-centered education") and the goal of academic planning for the next three to five years ("to improve the quality of QU's graduates"). With these aims in view, the groups were asked to generate a high-level planning charge for academic units. They determined that academic planning should address three overarching questions:

- What new initiatives could do the most to meet the mission and goal (e.g., new courses or programs, new majors or minors, new pedagogical styles and curricular materials)?
- What structures, processes, and resources (human, physical, administrative, financial) would be required to make the identified initiatives work?
- What criteria or metrics should be used for prioritizing choices and judging their success?

This charge was endorsed by the SRC and issued, essentially without alteration, by the head of the OIPD to all academic units in summer 2005, along with detailed guidance for the anticipated planning process. The planning effort itself—which was bottom-up—started at the departmental level. It took most of the 2005–2006 academic year to complete the three-year University-wide academic plan. Additionally, the core curriculum had yet to be fully developed by the project's end in January 2007.

At the end of the implementation project, a small number of departments had begun self-assessment exercises, benchmarking their academic programs against their peers regionally and internationally, as part of their regular review and planning processes. The College of Engineering and the College of Business had initiated the process of accreditation before the reform project began.[5] By the end of the reform project, the remaining colleges were exploring processes and mechanisms for reviewing their academic programs against discipline-based standards to ensure sustained improvement over time.

Improve Management of Faculty

Revitalized academic structures and services, described above, were expected to boost both faculty and student performance. The SRC and QU leadership took several additional steps to reinforce and reward faculty quality, as shown in Table 3.4.

Table 3.4
Improve Management of Faculty

Key Actions	Status as of January 2007
Develop, evaluate, and conduct faculty performance evaluations.	■
Develop longer-term contracts for expatriate faculty and staff.	■
Eliminate redundant faculty and staff.	■
Require and support faculty scholarly endeavors/research.	▨
Recruit/hire distinguished scholars in key areas.	▨
Revise retention and promotion policies.	□
Link retention of faculty and staff to performance evaluations.	□
Provide opportunities for and require pedagogical development.	□
Provide support to encourage effective sabbatic leaves.	□

■ Achieved   ▨ Partially achieved   □ In progress

---

[5] The College of Engineering was granted substantial equivalency accreditation by the Accreditation Board for Engineering and Technology (ABET) in 2005, and the College of Business started the process of accreditation with the Association to Advance Collegiate Schools of Business, expected in fall 2009.

In this domain, some structural and procedural changes were readily accomplished. A Faculty Performance Appraisal System involving quantitative and qualitative assessments, based on both overall QU academic priorities and faculty members' self-evaluations, was introduced by the University President in academic year 2005–2006, subjected to extensive formative evaluation, and revised on the basis of the results.[6] Further, expatriate contracting policies were revised to permit three-year rolling contracts (versus year-to-year contracts) for strong performers.

At the same time, efforts were being made both to hire new distinguished scholars in priority areas and to re-incentivize scholarship among existing faculty. While the development of new hiring policies and compensation schedules (see Table 3.1) had made it easier to attract desirable junior candidates, goals for the recruitment of distinguished faculty had not been met by the end of the implementation period.

Provision of generous intramural research funding through a newly established Office of Research encouraged faculty to undertake an increasing number of scholarly endeavors. These support opportunities, along with inclusion of scholarly endeavor in performance reviews, resulted in growing numbers of faculty research applications by the end of the implementation period; it was too soon, however, to assess their effects on faculty academic performance. Participation in professional pedagogical development was also being promoted, along with the use of existing sabbatical leave options to encourage longer-term professional scholarship undertakings.

Finally, efforts to increase the involvement of faculty working groups in academic program planning—with opportunities to craft new courses and redesign existing ones—were intended to result in increased ownership of and engagement in the academic enterprise across departments and colleges.

---

[6]   One of the early exercises in evidence-based decisionmaking, the formative evaluation undertaken by RQPI members of the project staff involved about 10 percent of QU faculty in confidential semi-structured interviews. Findings, distributed to all faculty as well as the SRC, became the basis for an improved faculty performance appraisal system. See Appendix E for further detail.

Among the changes recommended to improve faculty quality, revising retention and promotion policies and linking them to performance appraisal results was most challenging. In part, this difficulty was a carryover from the civil service system previously governing QU personnel decisionmaking. Under that system, promotion was largely dictated by amount of time served, and termination of Qatari nationals was unthinkable except in cases of gross malfeasance. However, it also reflected the Qatari culture: In practice, if not in law, Qatari nationals had virtually been guaranteed employment. These circumstances made mandatory separation, even for low-performing and unmotivated Qatari faculty, a painful prospect. Nonetheless, as Table 3.4 suggests, these difficult decisions were being made by QU leadership.

Foster and Support Student Achievement

The revitalized academic offerings discussed earlier were also intended to improve student academic performance. Early efforts to design the core curriculum emphasized inquiry-based learning, critical thinking, and problem solving and deemphasized rote retention. While welcoming these efforts, the SRC reminded the QU faculty that, at least in the view of the SRC, the objectives of the core curriculum went beyond developing essential skills. The core curriculum, they stressed, should also impart fundamental knowledge of the physical world and the human condition that underlies all academic pursuits. Supporting educational technologies and faculty professional development concurrently were intended to enable and enhance student-centered pedagogy. It was still necessary, however, to translate these reforms into improved student achievement (see Table 3.5).

The SRC recommended and QU leadership decided to begin changing performance standards for students by raising admissions and retention requirements. The University established stronger admissions requirements, for example, requiring the Test of English as a Foreign Language (TOEFL) examination and higher scores on the high school–leaving exams to be admitted directly into the University; otherwise, students would be required to enroll in the preparatory Foun-

Table 3.5
Foster and Support Student Achievement

Key Actions	Status as of January 2007
Strengthen and standardize admissions requirements.	■
Set minimum GPA standard for retention.	■
Codify and enforce academic regulations.	■
Expand and strengthen the Foundation Program.	■
Establish Office of Career Services.	■
Outreach to high schools to encourage adequate preparation for QU admission.	▨
Improve student advising and counseling.	▨
Develop honors recognition/courses/programs.	□

■ Achieved   ▨ Partially achieved   □ In progress

dation Program. Students whose grade point average (GPA) fell below 2.0 for one semester would be placed on probation for the following semester; three consecutive semesters with grades averaging below 2.0 would result in the student's suspension from the University. At the same time, the University took the decision to strengthen the Foundation Program to improve retention chances once students gained entrance to QU.[7]

The next steps in this reform domain included improving advising and counseling to current students about how to make academic progress and improving outreach to high school students contemplating future entry to QU. These efforts emphasized appropriate selection of a major field as well as the levels of prior preparation and ongoing effort commensurate with likely academic success in students' chosen majors. A career services office was also established to help students realize their longer-term employment goals.

---

[7] Data collected by the OIPD, with assistance from the reform project staff, suggested that highest student attrition occurred from the first to second year, probably as a result of inadequate prior preparation.

Finally, the SRC and QU leadership acknowledged that they had initially given their greatest attention to boosting the performance of students at the lower end of the achievement range. If the efforts to improve academic achievement among students succeeded, there should be reinforcing rewards for those attaining the upper achievement range as well. By the end of the reform implementation period, dean's honors lists were published each semester, and plans were in discussion to develop honors courses or programs.

Strengthen the University Community

The last domain of reform concerned strengthening the University "community." As Chapter Two describes, a general spirit of intellectual and collegial engagement in a shared mission of the institution was absent from QU when the reform project began. While strengthening the university community was not one of the major high-level recommendations made by the SRC, it was clear to the SRC that developing a community spirit and engagement would be vital to the overall success of the reform effort. The University President referred to giving new life to the University community as a "heart-and-soul" endeavor—one that would be critical to QU's ability to achieve and sustain its aspirations. While acknowledging the significant accomplishments represented by the creation of new organizational structures and procedures, the development of improved academic plans and programs, and the establishment of higher standards for students and faculty along with incentives to realize them, she argued that these were all necessary but not sufficient conditions for a revitalized community spirit.

Among the characteristics of such a community, the President cited a faculty that takes ownership of what it offers to students; academic leadership that combines energy, initiative, and devotion with responsibility, transparency, and accountability; and an environment that fosters initiative, creativity, and excellence. Admittedly, many of the items on this list are intangible qualities that are difficult to identify and assess; however, the SRC pinpointed some tangible indicators that enable the university to gauge its progress toward becoming a strengthened and cohesive university community. These are shown in Table 3.6.

The Vice President for Student Affairs declared academic year 2005–2006 to be the "year of the student" at QU. He and his staff introduced a comprehensive student orientation program, promoted a variety of extracurricular activities (many of them student-initiated and student-run), and engaged students in myriad other ways.

Student focus groups conducted by RQPI members of the reform project staff in spring 2006 revealed that students perceived considerable improvements in the quality of university life at QU, in spite of slow progress toward creating a physical environment more conducive to interpersonal interaction. Faculty focus groups, in contrast, continued to report longing for more community spirit and widened opportunities for collegial exchange. As Table 3.6 indicates, efforts to improve the physical and social infrastructure of QU are still in progress.

In the period from the inception to the conclusion of the implementation effort, however, regular communication about the nature and progress of the reform was maintained between QU leadership and the University's constituencies. With the QU External Relations Office taking the lead, a publication titled *Tawasol*, or *Communica-*

Table 3.6
Strengthen the University Community

Key Actions	Status as of January 2007
Introduce student orientation.	■
Promote student clubs/activities.	■
Improve infrastructure to provide students with common areas for socializing and studying.	▨
Improve library services and facilities.	▨
Develop activities that link faculty within and across departments (e.g., symposia, faculty club).	▨
Communicate University reform progress to University and beyond.	▨

■ Achieved   ▨ Partially achieved   ☐ In progress

tion in English, was being disseminated quarterly. Its initial issues were reform-themed, communicating information about the nature, spirit, and progress of the reform effort to the entire University community. In addition, efforts were underway to broaden communication between QU and wider public audiences. For example, the Vice President of Student Affairs hosted regular sessions called "Ask Dr. Omar" on the radio, where students and parents could call in and ask questions about changes occurring at the University. The University administrators also gave regular interviews to the press and frequently sent out press releases about the latest happenings at the University.

Looking Forward

The pace and extent of reform activity during the two-and-a-half-year implementation period were impressive. Noteworthy in the key action tables provided above is that none of the recommended reform initiatives was foregone entirely or halted in mid-course, in contrast to many organizational change efforts reported in the research literature. The SRC, at its final meeting, commended the University on the turnaround and the progress it had achieved.

Looking ahead to next steps at the end of the implementation project, the SRC offered two important, future-oriented suggestions. First, although QU had made systematic qualitative efforts to assess its reform actions, little was known about the ultimate outcomes of the changes that have taken place. The assumption behind the key actions is that successful implementation, as reflected in reaching the milestones, will add up to the creation of a high-quality institution. However, to establish solid evidence of success, more direct evaluation of outcomes is required. For this purpose, the SRC recommended that QU begin the process of identifying and collecting outcome measures in order to track and document performance improvements quantitatively over time. To this end, SRC members recommended that a prospective evaluation system be put in place by QU's OIPD. The IT system established to support academic progress tracking (see Table 3.3) would support the sorts of longitudinal, student-level analyses necessary to determine how well aims for improving student achievement were being met. Subsequently, QU leadership also initiated an Arabic translation of the National Survey of Student Engagement (NSSE) in order to track softer outcomes related to student involvement in the QU community.

Second, the SRC urged that QU continue its quest to become an exemplary higher education institution in the Gulf region, as the vision guiding the reform promises. By this, the SRC referred not just to sustaining the present accomplishments but also to embarking on future new directions that would build on and extend them, keeping the spirit of innovation alive at QU. Among the suggestions, several included course and program innovations—for instance, developing engaging "capstone" and/or interdisciplinary courses for upper-division students. The SRC also encouraged the exploration of good fits for interdisciplinary major-minor combinations. Other suggestions urged the development of centers or institutes that could provide research opportunities for faculty and students while fulfilling valuable social functions (e.g., an institute for public opinion research). The SRC emphasized that these inputs were intended to stimulate further dialog, and were by no means exhaustive of the types of new directions the University might contemplate.

CHAPTER FOUR

Reflections on the Reform: Key Elements of the Reform Strategy and Challenges to Implementation

In looking back at the Qatar University reform effort, there were important elements of the reform strategy that made accomplishing an ambitious agenda possible. In particular, the timing, sequencing, and leadership of the reform were key in supporting the difficult choices that the University leadership had to make along the path to reform. In this chapter, we review what, in retrospect, seem to have been important factors that contributed to achieving the reform's immediate objectives. This is followed by a discussion of some of the major tensions that the University faced in meeting its new mission. Our aim here is not to evaluate the ultimate outcomes of the reform. It is probably too early for such an assessment, and opinions will certainly differ on the extent of positive changes from the reform effort. Without a formal longitudinal evaluation, we cannot make definitive claims about how effective and lasting the changes will be. But we can reasonably argue that the reform met its own stated objectives, as outlined in the previous chapter. The principal changes specified in the reform agenda were carried out: The University established institutional autonomy and put in place policies and practices to improve decisionmaking, revitalize academic structures and services, improve faculty quality and student achievement, and finally, strengthen the University community. Whether these foundational changes are sufficiently institutionalized to survive beyond the current leadership of the University or withstand other pressures on the University's autonomy remains to be seen.

Conditions That Made Reform Possible

A confluence of events, conditions, and initial decisions by QU leaders made sweeping reform feasible. In retrospect, the following appear to have been particularly important.

Timing of the Reform

The reform of Qatar University began during a tide of change in Qatari society, when significant transformations in social roles, the education system, economy, and government institutions were occurring at a rapid rate. These sweeping changes in the country brought a sense of urgency and pressure on the University to respond seriously to the demands of the new environment. The reform effort benefited from the unprecedented opportunity to make such significant changes, some of which had been tried but failed at other times in the University's history. Although the experience of the University reform was challenging, and some may argue that it occurred too quickly, the momentum of the larger societal change helped to propel the University forward toward its intended vision and mission.

The Organization and Sequencing of the Reform

As we described in Chapter Three, structuring the reform project into phases over the two years of implementation proved to be an effective way to organize the work of the reform. It allowed for modular completion of reform project activities, which served as progress markers for the University. At the end of each phase, the SRC met to review progress and recommend adjustments and further activities that they saw as necessary to achieve the goals of the reform. This gave the reformers the opportunity to step back from the day-to-day activities of implementation and to take a comprehensive view of what was being accomplished. These regular pauses for reflection and readjustment were valuable in keeping key activities on track. As just one example, early in the implementation phase, it was evident from discussions at an SRC meeting that the Faculty Performance Appraisal System needed significant adjustment to address imbalances in the measures and weighting of items in faculty evaluations. Based on the information presented by

University staff at the meeting, the SRC recommended that the reform project staff undertake a formative evaluation of the Faculty Performance Appraisal System to determine where the problems were and how the system might be adjusted. Based on the evaluation presented at the next meeting, the SRC recommended several changes to the system for the next cycle, which were subsequently implemented.

The sequencing of the reform activities also proved to be tactically astute. The reform effort began by first changing the organizational and administrative structures of the University to give the QU leadership the autonomy and flexibility it needed to make the hundreds of detailed operational changes necessary at all levels of the University. Importantly, His Highness the Emir initiated the reform by using his authority as Supreme Head of the University one final time to grant QU independence from the Ministry of Finance and Ministry of Civil Service Affairs and Housing. This was a critical move for the University. Otherwise, the University leadership believes, the reform would never have happened. Without the freedom granted by the Emir to manage its own budget plans, spending, and personnel policies, QU could not have overcome inertia and resistance in the ministries.

Immediately following the structural changes, new University administrative policies and procedures were established. The University leadership believed that introducing systems of accountability and standardizing policies and practices were vital next steps after the organizational changes. As the University president said,

> The reform put in place accountability, and began to put an end to the chaos that dominated the University's operations before. Many people liked the chaotic ways of doing things because they benefited from it; no one really knew what was going on, so people could take advantage of others' ignorance.[1]

The new policies and procedures put in place standards for how the University would operate, by which everyone in the University community would have to abide. These fundamental organizational and

---

[1] Interview with President Sheikha Al Misnad, June 2008.

administrative changes were necessary to create the foundation for all the other operational changes that needed to take place at QU. Of course, lasting reform requires changes in the fundamental attitudes, daily habits, and patterns of academic life, but these can happen only with time, as the University community internalizes the cultural changes and institutionalizes them. This process is still ongoing at the University.

Strong Leadership

Even with effective organization and sequencing, the reform effort would likely have stalled without the well-supported leadership of the President of Qatar University, Sheikha Al Misnad. First, the President had the support and confidence of the higher authorities to undertake the reform: His Highness the Emir gave the President the necessary authority and resources. But with the authority and resources came responsibility for introducing the reform to the University community. She had to motivate the faculty and staff to participate in the reform and accept the change, while addressing the negative reaction from both the internal QU community and the broader external community. In particular, the changes to the GPA standards, faculty performance evaluation and compensation schemes, and changes to the University's college and department structure caused uncertainty and confusion among some in the QU community.

As important as strong leadership at the top was, much depended on the layers below the top administration to carry out key implementation activities. Strong college, department, and program leadership has been essential to ensure the reforms are viable and lasting. Many, if not most, of the reforms came together at the level of the academic departments. Department heads suddenly found themselves with significant new responsibilities for academic planning, budgeting, and faculty performance appraisal, among others. At the time the reform plans were being developed, the burden that would fall on the department heads was not well understood, and many of the department heads were not ready for their new responsibilities. Indeed, lower levels of academic leadership had atrophied in the years prior to the reform, so finding the right people to take on these new responsibilities was a serious challenge. Considerable time was spent in the beginning of the reform on finding the right people to put in place as departmental leaders. Despite training opportunities, many department heads felt they were not given the additional support and assistance needed to carry out their new tasks.

The University as Primary Actor

From the beginning of the reform, both RQPI and the University leadership understood that QU had to reform itself if the effort was to be successful and enduring. As one QU member of the Senior Reform Committee noted, the reform project could not be performed by a "consultant magician who would come do his magic at the University and leave. . . . We realized from day one that it was *our* project. We were involved with everything." The structure of the reform project was designed to put the University in the lead of every aspect of the effort. Importantly, the SRC was composed of senior members of the QU faculty and administration and supplemented with outside experts with significant experience in higher education leadership and management. The SRC was supported by RQPI and QU reform project staffs who worked together to carry out research, analyses, and implementation activities recommended by the SRC.

Also significant, after the first year, the QU reform project staff was led by the OIPD, which coordinated the various reform implementation activities and ensured that the implementation moved forward steadily. As one SRC member noted, the OIPD acted as the "guardian of the reform." The OIPD followed the development and execution of decisions made by the University leadership and ensured that there was follow-through on key reform activities. The OIPD offered important internal guidance on implementation questions and helped to "sell" the reform to the University community by communicating with faculty and staff about the reform plan and working with them on the various implementation activities. Placing this office at the center of the reform activities and in charge of implementation helped maintain the momentum of the reform.

Support from Outside Experts

The reform benefited from strong relationships between senior members of the University and experienced outside advisors and specialized consultants. The QU leadership knew that it could not carry out the reform on its own; it needed outside help to develop the vision and strategies for change, as well as supplementary technical expertise to carry them out.

SRC members—those from the University and those from outside—were chosen to create a balanced group with complementary expertise. Once the SRC members had been selected, strong support from both the Emir and Her Highness provided assurance to the members of the seriousness and commitment to the reform from the highest levels of government.

Beginning in the first year of the reform, members of the SRC built a strong rapport and level of trust that continued to strengthen over the next two years of implementation. The majority of these same members worked together throughout the three years of the project. The rapport and trust among members of the SRC allowed them to work together effectively. SRC meetings were characterized by open, constructive discussion and debate. Disagreements on various issues were common, but there was an atmosphere of respect and tolerance for different perspectives. The QU members of the SRC benefited from the external members who served as a "sounding board" for ideas and questions and who provided reassurance and confidence that the reform initiatives could work. The external members of the SRC benefited from the opportunity to build close relationships with the QU members and to get to know the institution, which allowed them to put their ideas and recommendations into context.

Although the SRC members' time together was limited, it was well used. The reform project staff members worked together to set up issues for SRC discussion, so that meetings were well organized and sharply focused on the important issues at hand. The SRC members noted that having project staff in residence in Doha on a continuous basis to support the effort was critical to keeping the SRC informed and connected to the implementation activities of the University between meetings.

The University also benefited from technical and specialized consultants who were brought in to supplement the reform project staff. In addition to the RQPI team, consultants were hired directly by the University to work on specialized projects, such as business systems development, a student information system, and development of the core curriculum. In all cases, the emphasis of this external assistance was on building knowledge "on the ground" and using consultants to support the efforts of the University leadership and management rather than outsourcing project implementation. Thus, the University was able to get the best out of the outside consultants and experts without ceding control of decisionmaking or implementation.

The Difficult Choices

Establishing and then implementing the reform agenda forced the QU leadership to make some difficult choices. Perhaps all universities face some versions of these choices, but the particular circumstances of Qatar University and the character of Qatari society made the choices especially stark.

Academic Standards Versus Social Norms

In the years before the reforms, many members of Qatari society viewed admission to and graduation from the national university as a privilege routinely available to all nationals. Academic standards—for both admission and graduation—were not rigorous. About half of the Qatari nationals graduating from secondary schools qualified for free admission to QU, and a GPA of only 1.5 (out of a maximum possible 4.0) was sufficient for continued enrollment in and eventual graduation from the University. In addition, the University's Parallel Program opened an additional route for admission and graduation to students who did not meet the standard admissions criteria and were willing to pay tuition.

At the time the University reforms began, efforts to strengthen secondary education in Qatar were in their early phases and had not yet borne fruit in the form of increased numbers of students prepared to undertake rigorous, academically oriented university studies. Qatar's school-leaving examinations were not benchmarked against international standards, but less formal indicators suggested that Qatari high school graduates were, on average, not well prepared for university studies. Few graduates from state-run high schools, for example, were qualified for admission to universities in the United States, Europe, or Australia without additional preparation. Furthermore, opportunities for such additional preparation were limited. The Qatar Foundation's Academic Bridge Program could accommodate only limited numbers of students seeking admission to Western universities, and QU's foundation programs were available only to students entering the College of Science and the College of Engineering.

A new vocational college—the College of the North Atlantic—had opened in Doha, but there were few alternatives to QU for less qualified students or for students whose education had been interrupted and who now sought academically oriented post-secondary studies. There was, for example, no institution in Qatar similar to an American community college, which offers alternative pathways to employment or further education for these types of students.[2]

In these circumstances, QU faced considerable social pressure to be all things to all students, providing opportunities for continuing education for large numbers of young Qataris who might not be well prepared for university studies. Simply put, there was no alternative to QU.

At that time as well, significant reform of the Qatari civil service still lay in the future. Government positions were and remain the preferred employment option for most Qataris. Overstaffing of government agencies was endemic at that time, and civil service jobs were plentiful for Qatari nationals. There was no effective review of job performance in the public sector, and poorly performing government employees were seldom dismissed. Moreover, civil service employment policies allowed no differentiation in starting salaries among college graduates on the basis of fields of study or academic performance during their

---

[2] As of 2009, there still is no community college or similar institution, although planning for one is under way.

university careers. For many civil service positions, the only meaningful requirement was a university degree—in any field and with any grades. Consequently, Qatari university students had few incentives to pursue challenging courses of study or to work hard for better grades. In this environment, QU faced strong social pressure to allow large numbers of less-than-motivated students to graduate.

The first hard choices QU had to face in shaping its reform agenda related to its academic mission: Whom should QU teach, what should it teach, and what should it demand of its graduates?

The SRC recommended and His Highness the Emir subsequently agreed that QU could not be expected to meet all of Qatar's needs for post-secondary education. QU would aim to serve average and above-average Qataris who seek academically oriented university education. Further, there would be a single standard for admission to QU, and the Parallel Program should be eliminated.

The QU leadership recognized that this choice would leave gaps in Qatar's post-secondary education system. In particular, the role played in other countries by community colleges would be at least temporarily unfilled. But the SRC and QU leadership argued that the task of providing good-quality, academically oriented education to qualified students was sufficiently challenging to absorb all of the University's energies. Other roles in post-secondary education would be left to other institutions, some yet to be created.

The SRC recognized, however, that preparation for university studies provided by Qatar's secondary schools would remain inadequate for some years to come. Thus, the SRC recommended that QU's Foundation Program be expanded to accommodate all applicants willing to work diligently to qualify for university studies. Scores on the school-leaving examination required for admission to QU had been raised shortly before the formal beginning of the reform process. Although this action encountered significant resistance from the larger community, the University persevered. No further formal tightening of admissions criteria was enacted, but all students without necessary qualifications were routed into the expanded Foundation Program.

Improved academic achievement by students who were admitted to QU was a major objective of the reform. Early in the reform process, the GPA required for continuing enrollment and graduation was raised from 1.5 to 2.0. This action, too, faced considerable community opposition. The University also began work on other endeavors that were intended to generate and support a more rigorous academic experience for its undergraduates. It developed a core curriculum intended to instill fundamental intellectual and communication skills and humanistic and scientific literacy. Academic regulations were codified and enforced. Student orientation and academic advising were strengthened. In making these decisions, the University leadership accepted that graduation rates might drop, at least temporarily, but felt that establishment of meaningful standards was essential to the University's academic integrity.

Pragmatism Versus Ambition

Among the difficult choices that the leadership of QU faced as it began the reform process was balancing what was realistically achievable and valuable to Qatar in the near-term against the grander visions of what the University could and should become in the future. Some members of the University faculty favored ambitious programs—postgraduate degrees, sharply expanded funding for research, and efforts to attract the best students from all over the region, for example. Others argued for more-limited objectives, concentrating on good undergraduate education for Qatari nationals who could not or did not wish to attend foreign universities.

The State of Qatar aspires to become a major center for intellectual, cultural, and scientific activity in the Middle East. This aspiration, however, does not necessarily imply that the national university must seek similar stature—at least in the next several years. Other institutions in the country—branch campuses of foreign universities, specialized research centers, Qatar-based organizations drawing international participation, and so on—can all contribute to the State's larger aspirations.

The SRC recommended a pragmatic approach, with objectives that could realistically be achieved within a few years. In particular, the SRC urged that QU should remain primarily an undergraduate institution. They also recognized that, by remaining primarily an undergraduate institution without significant numbers of postgraduate students, the University could not pursue academic research—at least as such research is typically conducted at major universities. Partly for this reason, the SRC chose to emphasize a somewhat broader concept of "scholarly endeavor"—which would include traditional university research, pedagogical innovation, and various other forms of intellectually rigorous inquiry—as essential to the University's life. These all could be pursued within an undergraduate setting.

The SRC also recognized that particularly well-qualified Qatari students would and should continue to seek university education abroad or in the foreign university branch campuses of Education City. QU, they urged, should structure itself to meet the needs of the large majority of Qatari students, for whom foreign education is not available or appropriate. Further, QU should concentrate its resources on the disciplines most immediately valuable in Qatar—engineering and business, for example—while deemphasizing, at least temporarily, some subjects that might be intellectually elegant but of less practical application in Qatar's current and likely future circumstances.

Despite these emphases, the reform agenda included provisions for more ambitious expansion of University programs in later years. New mechanisms for funding and managing research, for example, were put in place. Small departments devoted to "pure sciences" (in which enrollment had been low for several years) were consolidated for organizational efficiency, but they were not abolished. These departments can be expanded later, as circumstances and student demand require. Although QU must serve the large majority of young Qataris seeking university education, the SRC recommended that QU establish an honors college to provide special services to outstanding students who, for one reason or another, cannot or do not wish to attend foreign universities.

Well-Established Versus Innovative Academic Structures

A key challenge that the designers of QU's reform faced was to devise an overall academic structure for the University that would support the goals of devolving academic responsibility to academic departments and colleges and of developing and delivering a new core curriculum to be required of all QU graduates. The SRC devoted considerable time and energy to debating alternative models for the academic structure of the reformed University.

One model featured a central College of Arts and Sciences, which would combine into a single college the existing College of Humanities and Social Science and College of Science. The new CAS would have primary responsibility for developing and delivering the core curriculum, as well as offering its own degree programs in appropriate fields. The CAS would be surrounded by five "professional" colleges—Engineering, Education, Business, Law, and Sharia.

The SRC saw this option as reflecting a well-established model for higher education, successfully implemented at such leading universities as Harvard and the University of Michigan. The SRC noted that the breadth of the new college would allow it to develop virtually the entire core curriculum from within its academic departments, providing students with solid grounding in literature, social studies, mathematics, and science. But the SRC worried that a CAS might be so large and heterogeneous as to be unmanageable. They suggested, though, that this risk might be mitigated through efforts to break down artificial divisions among degree programs and to consolidate academic departments where student demand was weak.

An alternative model would place responsibility for the core curriculum with the existing College of Humanities and Social Sciences, with the expectation that leaders of that college would reach out to other colleges for necessary core courses in mathematics and sciences. The College of Engineering and the College of Science would be combined into a single College of Engineering and Science. Colleges of Education, Business, Law, and Sharia would remain independent.

The principal motivation for this structure was recognition that boundaries between science and engineering are becoming increasingly artificial. In the modern world, advances in either of these fields reinforce advances in the other. Also, because mathematics and basic sciences are prerequisites for all engineering degree programs, some efficiencies and synergies would likely result from locating the departments responsible for such courses in the same college as engineering departments. The SRC acknowledged a risk that this combination might distract the already strong College of Engineering from its pursuit of international accreditation.

At a more fundamental level, the choice between these two models came down to a choice between reinforcing strengths that QU already had and trying to share those strengths more broadly within the University. The Colleges of Science and Engineering were both strong and reform-minded. Courses in both colleges were already taught in English. Both had high proportions of faculty who had earned advanced degrees at Western universities. These faculty understood and valued the Western approach to higher education and research. And the College of Engineering was already well advanced on its path to international accreditation. Combining these two strong colleges would arguably strengthen both. But it would leave a comparatively weak College of Humanities and Social Sciences—still teaching in Arabic and with many faculty from traditionally oriented regional universities—unable to deliver a successful core curriculum.

Ultimately, the SRC recommended adopting the first approach, the better-established model of a central College of Arts and Sciences. The Committee recognized that QU still had major reforms to accomplish before it might benefit fully from the advantages of more closely integrating science and engineering. It was not lost on the Committee that the universities that had made this model work were among the most advanced and sophisticated technically oriented schools in the world. Perhaps QU was not yet ready for such a bold design. Even more important, however, was the hope that the reform-oriented attitudes prevalent in the College of Science would be transferred to the new CAS and would therefore guide development of the core curriculum. Indeed, the first dean of the CAS was a mathematician drawn from the former College of Science.

University Service Versus Scholarly Development

Perhaps the most poignant decision that the QU leadership faced in implementing the reform agenda was assignment of some promising younger faculty members to fill key administrative positions within the University—deans, department heads, academic planners, etc.

For a number of reasons, these younger faculty were obvious choices for administrative posts. Many had received advanced degrees from Western universities and therefore gained valuable exposure to policies and practices at those institutions. Because they were relative newcomers to QU, they were often less attached to older ways of doing things and more open to change.

The problem was that these promising young scholars were diverted from building their own academic careers: Papers were not written, new courses were not developed, research interests were not pursued. These faculty members' willingness to take on administrative duties at a crucial period in the University's history came at considerable cost to their own development as scholars. The University also bore a cost, in the sense that it was mortgaging a part of its future—some of its best young faculty—in order to meet the immediate needs of the reform.

The President of the University recognized and agonized over this sacrifice. But ultimately, she had little choice. The senior faculty ranks simply did not include enough people with the right skills or attitudes to implement the reforms. Only by sacrificing—all hoped temporarily—the scholarly development of the young, open-minded faculty could the University proceed with the reforms.

The Pace of Reform

The pace of reform during the first two years of implementation was very rapid. Perhaps the most dramatic example of this rapid pace was the merging of the College of Humanities and the College of Sciences into the new College of Arts and Sciences. The Emir approved this change in structure in June 2004. The new college was in operation the following September. Also with the beginning of the 2004–2005 academic year, responsibility for personnel decisions and budget planning devolved to heads of academic departments. New, higher academic standards—the minimum GPA required for continued enrollment and new terms of academic probation—were also introduced in the fall of 2004. The Board of Regents was recruited during the summer following the Emir's approval, and the Board met for the first time in November 2004. The new Faculty Performance Appraisal System had been tested on a pilot basis even before the Emir approved the reform agenda and was in operation during the 2004–2005 academic year. And while the University community was digesting all of these changes, work was under way on designing the first core curriculum, writing manuals of policies and procedures, creating new financial management systems, establishing an Office of Research, organizing new student orientation and counseling services, and initiating systematic academic planning.

Not surprisingly, the University paid a price for proceeding so rapidly. For example, the combination of the College of Humanities and the College of Science (and the consolidation of some academic departments within these colleges) took place with little preparation or advance notice for affected faculty. The result was considerable confusion and some resistance to the change. Heads of academic departments were generally not prepared to assume their new responsibilities for personnel management and budget planning, and the University did not initially have resources in place to support the department heads with these responsibilities. Some department heads resisted the changes, and personnel policies and budget planning were in some disarray during the first academic year of reform implementation. Parents and students protested the new standards for GPAs, complaining that these had been imposed without adequate warning. And the Faculty Performance Appraisal System had to be revamped significantly after pilot testing. The small circle of administrators most directly involved in managing the reforms were also stretched to the limit of their capabilities.

QU leaders were aware of the difficulties inherent in moving rapidly, but they also saw advantages in doing so. The most significant of these was that the rapid pace left little time for opposition to the reforms—within the University itself or within the larger community— to become entrenched. Also, the rapid pace created a sort of reform momentum, as progress in one area required or facilitated progress in others. A general sense that the process of reform was moving forward on multiple fronts had the effect of spurring efforts across the full range of reform activities. The Emir's approval of the reform plan gave the QU leadership the authority necessary to proceed with the reform, and it acted on this authority as quickly as possible.

In retrospect, the QU President and other leaders of the reform believe that the choice to proceed rapidly was correct. The major structural and procedural reforms had to be solidly and irrevocably in place to create an environment conducive to longer-term behavioral and attitudinal changes.

Efficiency Versus Inclusiveness

The ultimate success of reforms at QU—or at any university for that matter—depend on acceptance of the principles and the specific character of the reform by faculty, staff, and students. A broadly inclusive approach to reform that invites participation of the university community in the processes of establishing and implementing the reform agenda may speed this acceptance. But an inclusive approach can also give a voice to elements within the university who oppose change, opening the door to endless debate and possibly stalling the reform process entirely.

The QU leadership recognized that some elements of the QU faculty were likely to oppose key parts of the reform. Opposition in particular quarters would hardly have been surprising, given the sweeping nature of the reform. The leadership also realized, though, that successful implementation of the hundreds of operational decisions that would make reform a practical reality would require a cadre of faculty and staff with thorough understanding of the objectives of the reform and dedication to its success.

Consequently, the leadership chose a compromise between restricting influence over the reform to a small inner circle and opening the process to the entire University community. The President appointed sympathetic and respected faculty—at first just a handful— to the reform project staff that supported the deliberations of the Senior Reform Committee. These faculty had full access to the discussions of the SRC and played key roles in gathering the background information necessary to formulate the agenda. Their views were solicited during SRC meetings, but they were asked to hold confidential the discussions that took place among the members of the SRC. This group formed the beginnings of a cadre of influential and supportive faculty who would lead the reform forward.

As implementation of the reform agenda began, additional supportive faculty were invited to join the reform project staff. Other faculty and staff were assigned responsibility for specific tasks—for example, beginning the design of the core curriculum, drafting new policies for managing research at the University, or refining the Faculty Performance Appraisal System. Those invited to join in implementation of the reforms were chosen from among faculty and staff who were broadly supportive of the reform objectives. By no means did this selection result in unanimity of views about important elements of the reform. The implementation phase of the reform was marked by spirited but constructive debate about specific operational choices. This debate, though, took place within a gradually expanding circle of faculty and staff, all committed to the principles of the reform. Key reform actions were announced to the general University community only once they were clearly decided and implementation was under way. The University leadership made a specific decision to postpone creation of a faculty senate until the major structural and institutional aspects of the reform had been completed.

This approach was not without costs. The fact that a reform process was under way was not, of course, a secret. In the absence of authoritative information about the reform, rumors and misrepresentations circulated. Some faculty felt excluded from important decisions affecting the University, and some indeed left the University.

There is, of course, no way of knowing whether a more inclusive process might have brought better or faster results. Neither can we know whether the changes in attitudes and behaviors that will be essential to the sustained success of the reform have been advanced or hindered by the particular approach chosen. The University leadership does not, however, regret its choice. It was inevitable, in its view, that some parts of the faculty would never accept the necessary reforms. These voices were not permitted to derail the reform process, and their departure was arguably beneficial both to the University and to the faculty members themselves.

CHAPTER FIVE

The Challenges Ahead

Universities are living institutions, and no change—whether positive or negative—is necessarily permanent. It has been four years since the QU reform was launched, and already some of the academic structures, academic programs, and operating policies envisioned in the original reform agenda are being adjusted. Significantly, though, these adjustments are originating from within an autonomous, self-governing University. The adjustments have been proposed from the University's own planning apparatus and, when necessary, approved by the University's Board of Regents. The University's ability to change and adapt in this way, without reference to outside authorities or ministries, would not have been possible before the reforms and is itself among the most significant accomplishments of the reform.

The major structural and organizational objectives of the reform have been achieved, but these have not yet been fully institutionalized. The administration that conceived and implemented the reforms is still largely in place. The next major test for the reforms will come when this administration is replaced by a new generation. Only then will we see the extent to which the principles of the reform have been firmly embedded in the University's institutional structure and are not dependent on the energy and vision of a few individuals.

Some years will also be required to establish the independence of the University in national custom and practice. No public university is or can be completely autonomous. The state that provides the bulk of a public university's financial resources has legitimate interests in how those resources are spent and in the character of the service that the university provides to the larger community. But long experience has shown that a successful university needs significant operational auton-omy, within its broad public mandate and consistent with its budget-ary resources. There is always a tension—not necessarily undesirable or unconstructive—between government officials responsible for the prudent use of public resources and the administrations of public uni-versities charged with serving the educational, scientific, and cultural interests of the nation. Inevitably, government officials seek occasion-ally to exert more or different influence over the operations of a uni-versity. And inevitably, university administrators seek to defend their independence.

QU's operational independence from government ministries is of only a few years standing at this point. The University has already seen what it regards as some attempts to encroach upon its operational autonomy. This is not surprising, and it will be only over the course of some years—and probably new generations of leadership on both sides—that government agencies and the University define their appro-priate roles and spheres of influence. This process will require patience, goodwill, and vigilance on the part of all concerned.

At the end of the formal reform project, the most pressing aca-demic challenge remaining was completion of the core curriculum. The University was still working to achieve an appropriate balance between imparting the fundamental knowledge necessary for a liberal education and developing the particular skills necessary for academic success. More broadly, the University must complete the realignment of faculty and student attitudes, expectations, and behaviors that the reform at QU has begun. Already, University leaders see a new accep-tance of accountability and recognition of individual responsibility throughout the University. Ultimately, the character of the University will be determined and guaranteed by its faculty and its students, not by its administrators, its organizational structures, or its bylaws. The QU reforms have succeeded in changing the structural and organi-zational aspects of the University, and they have prompted the begin-nings of what the University leadership consider positive changes in the less formal and less easily controlled spirit of the University. Complet-ing and sustaining these latter changes are challenging tasks and still mostly lie ahead.

Senior Reform Committee Members

Qatar University Members of the SRC

Omar M. Al Ansari	*Vice President for Student Affairs*
Humaid Abdulla Al Midfaa	*Vice President and Chief Financial Officer*
Sheikha Abdulla Al Misnad	*President, University of Qatar*
Fathy Sauod	*Professor of Parasitology, University of Qatar; Advisor on Higher Education to the Qatar Foundation*
Noura Al Subaai	*Vice President and Chief Academic Officer (2004–2005)*
Shaikha Jabor Al Thani	*Dean, College of Arts and Sciences (2004–2005); Vice President and Chief Academic Officer (2005–present)*

External Members of the SRC

Roger W. Benjamin	*President, Council for Aid to Education*

Kenneth H. Keller	*Director, Center for Science, Technology, and Public Policy of the Hubert H. Humphrey Institute of Public Affairs of the University of Minnesota; former President of the University of Minnesota*
Jane L. Lightfoot	*Sherwood Fellow and Tutor in Classical Languages and Literature, New College, Oxford, New College, Oxford*
Marvin W. Peterson	*Professor of Higher Education, University of Michigan; former Director of the Center for the Study of Higher and Post-secondary Education, University of Michigan*
Daniel P. Resnick	*Special Assistant for Academic Affairs to the President of Carnegie Mellon University; former Chairman of the Faculty Senate, Carnegie Mellon University*

Qatar University's Vision and Mission Statements

Vision

Qatar University seeks to be a model national university that offers high quality, learning-centered education to its students.

Mission

To promote the cultural and scientific development of the Qatari society while preserving its Arabic characteristics and maintaining its Islamic cultural heritage. The University's dissemination of knowledge shall contribute to the development and advancement of human thought and values. The University shall provide the country with specialists, technicians, and experts in various fields, and equip citizens with knowledge and advanced research methodologies. The University shall also remain committed to strengthening its scientific and cultural ties with other Arab and international universities and educational institutions.

Conceptual Framework for the Qatar University Reform Project

The conceptual framework guiding this project reflects a line of research developed at RAND and elsewhere in the 1970s that views educational reform as a type of organizational innovation.[1] The framework conceptualizes successful organizational innovation as a function of three classes of variables, outlined below in relation to the QU reform project.

- *Features of the innovation to be undertaken.* The reform project began by articulating a new vision of QU as a model national university offering high-quality, learning-centered education and drawing out its implications in a mission statement (see Appendix B).
- *Innovation-relevant characteristics of the organization and its broader institutional environment.* After setting out the vision and mission, the project turned its attention to identifying characteristics of QU and its context that could pose obstacles to realizing the envisioned reform (e.g., lack of institutional autonomy, absence of a culture of achievement among students). At the same time, the project sought to build on QU's extant strengths (e.g., strongly committed top leadership, plentiful resources).
- *Implementation, or the process by which the innovative change is introduced and embedded in the pre-existing setting.* The implemen-

---

[1] See especially the work of Berman et al. (1977) and Pressman and Wildavsky (1979), as well as Bardach (1980), Fullan and Pomfret (1977), and Guba and Lincoln (1982).

tation process, construed here as the myriad decisions made and actions taken over time to carry out the reform agenda, formed the focus for the last two years of this three-year project. Across varied types of public and private sector organizations, prior research converges on the conclusion that variables representing the quality of the implementation process are the strongest predictors of successful innovation. Among these indicators, involvement of those who will be affected by the changes in the decisions and actions that direct them is most strongly associated with positive outcomes.

Finally, the framework as employed here adopts a "mutual adaptation" rather than a "fidelity" conception of success.[2] That is, the envisioned reform is not treated as a blueprint for change that ends in success when the blueprint is faithfully realized. Rather, success is seen as the continuous adaptation of the organization to achieve the aims of the reform, even as specific features of the reform are adapted to better fit the changing organization and its contest. Given this view of success, the critical part played by stakeholders' participatory involvement in the implementation process is their role in linking commitment to the innovation with knowledge about the way the organization works and how to change it.

---

[2]   See summaries of this orientation in the work of Bikson and Eveland (1991), as well as Rice and Rogers (1980), Tornatzky et al. (1980, 1983), Tornatzky and Johnson (1982), and Yin et al. (1976, 1978).

An Exercise in Decentralized Planning and Decisionmaking: Developing a University-Wide Academic Plan

Origin and Purpose

Once Qatar University established its new vision and mission, the SRC recommended that the University undertake a university-wide academic planning process. This was an especially crucial next step, because the goals of the institution had changed significantly and the newly restructured administrative offices, colleges, and departments were in need of a cohesive sense of direction.

Although academic planning was an effective way to tackle a number of necessary academic reforms, the chief goal of the planning effort was to *improve the quality of QU graduates*. To that end, the academic planning process was aimed at three important outcomes:

- Develop a detailed plan for the next three years of University operations.
- Require all academic units to identify their most important priorities.
- Introduce faculty and administrators to a system of evidence-based decisionmaking that relies upon shared criteria, standard methods of evaluation, and institution-wide deliberation.

The Process

During the course of the 2005–2006 academic year, every academic unit within Qatar University—as well as the library, student services, and other related offices—was asked to submit an academic plan.

The academic planning process was designed to be iterative and collaborative, with an emphasis on a bottom-up approach. Indeed, the process began with a focus group study to gather faculty input on the development of the academic planning framework and solicit their opinions about how the process should be carried out. The academic administration adopted the recommendations generated by the study, and faculty suggestions were incorporated into the final planning approach.

Since this was a new undertaking for the University, the administration recognized that the process would not be successful without targeted outreach and support for faculty and staff. Therefore, representatives from the OIPD conducted instructional workshops about the planning process and the required documents, worked with unit representatives responsible for developing plans to guide them through the process, and communicated with the broader University community about the purpose of this endeavor.

Representatives from the various academic units participated on an Academic Planning Task Force that reviewed the planning documents submitted by the units, provided feedback on the goals and action plans, and suggested a number of institution-wide priorities that would address the areas most in need of development and support. Once these priorities were reviewed and accepted by the Executive Management Committee (EMC) and the Board of Regents, the OIPD developed an action plan that laid out the steps necessary to carry out the academic plan. The OIPD also identified key performance indicators and target deadlines for meeting the University-wide and unit-specific priorities and oversaw adjustments to the plans deemed necessary because of new developments or altered circumstances.

Components of the Plan

Each academic unit was asked to submit a planning document that included the following components:

1. A mission statement that captures the role of that unit within QU
2. A statement of goals and objectives that takes into consideration issues such as: academic offerings, innovative initiatives that support the University's new vision and mission, and faculty and student needs
3. A realistic plan to meet those goals
4. A supplement to that plan that indicates how additional resources would be used to strengthen existing programs and support new programs of the highest priority
5. Any supporting documents and statistical evidence that bolster the legitimacy and reasonableness of the plan.

The fifth component required that the University develop a statistical database that could provide units with necessary information for planning, including enrollment and attrition rates, student/faculty ratios, and resource distribution and use. Since this database was still being created during the 2005–2006 academic year, it was acknowledged that there would be gaps in the data provided by the academic units; in such cases, unit leaders were simply asked to indicate those holes and to do what they could to provide any relevant empirical information that could assist in the assessment of their plans.

Criteria for Review

Five criteria were applied by the Academic Planning Task Force to evaluate the various aspects of the academic plans:

- *Quality.* Inevitably a subjective measure, this criterion focuses on the quality of faculty teaching, research, and service (as reflected in publications and measures of teaching effectiveness), as well as the quality of students, academic offerings, resources, library collections, and so on.

- *Centrality:* Each program should be evaluated in terms of its contribution to QU's mission. Specifically, they should be considered in terms of the degree to which the program is an essential component of a challenging liberal, preprofessional, or professional education. Another issue to consider as a part of this criterion consider is the extent to which it instills an understanding of the major ideas and achievements of mankind as well as a particular awareness of the values of Qatar's own culture, tradition, and intellectual heritage.

- *Demand and workload.* Both short- and long-term demands (including those that are stable or expected to decline) for each program should be considered with this criterion in mind. Demand indicators might include applicant rates, services performed in support of other programs, the number of courses offered, ongoing research projects, contributions toward the solution pressing societal problems, and the prospective market for graduates. If a program has suffered a substantial decline in workload, the program should be asked to justify its existence and its budget.

- *Cost-effectiveness.* Because aspirations are always limited by the resources available, programs must be regularly examined to see if more economical or more efficient tactics are possible to accomplish the same ends. However, considerations of cost alone must not govern this criterion; the effectiveness of the program as a whole must also be weighed. When taken together, cost and effectiveness provide an important measure of whether funds are being put to the best use.

- *Comparative advantage.* Another inherently subjective measure, assessment within this criterion should be driven by such questions as What is the rationale for this program at QU? What are the unique characteristics of each program that make it essential to the nation and/or other University programs?

Final Recommendations

Although the first round of academic planning was viewed positively by the SRC, the Committee expressed concerns regarding the ambitious number of priorities and tasks that were amassed in the unit and University-wide plans by the end of the 2005–2006 academic year. Their recommendations therefore focused on how QU could implement its three-year academic plan as successfully and efficiently as possible. This included the following advice:

- Ensure the action plans are organized appropriately and distributed accurately across the University's offices and academic units.
- Select a few initiatives from the action plan to be accomplished in the first year of implementation. Preference should be given to items that will have an immediate and tangible effect on the quality of life for the faculty and students at QU.
- Incorporate faculty more directly in the work of implementing the academic plans. Not only will this increase the faculty's sense of investment in the changes that will be taking place, but the University also stands to benefit from the diverse range of knowledge and insights the faculty have to share.
- Clarify the criteria to be used in reviewing academic programs. Since the aforementioned criteria for review may be interpreted and weighed relative to one another in a diverse range of ways, it is important to establish a clear understanding of *how* these criteria will be used to determine which programs should receive additional support, which should be downsized or phased out, and which should be newly established.
- Learn from the academic planning experience, especially in terms of how to carry out multilevel University-wide decisionmaking. Examples of such lessons include improving communication with all stakeholders, clarifying expectations, and providing a uniform and consistent set of practice guidelines.
- As implementation moves from one year to the next, evaluate the success of the process itself. Review the progress made by posing

such questions such as Has real change happened? What did the people involved learn from this process? How should QU use its resources to ensure it reaches the intended academic planning goals?

These recommendations were embraced by the administration, and they continue to guide the ongoing efforts to implement the plan and uphold the University's academic priorities.

Improving Faculty Development and Accountability: The Faculty Performance Appraisal System

Origin and Purpose

In the 2004–2005 academic year, under the purview of the Office of Academic Evaluation and the Office of Faculty and Instructional Development, a Faculty Performance Appraisal System (FPAS) was launched for University-wide deployment. The development of appraisal procedures had been recommended by the SRC in its June 2004 report on reforming Qatar University. From the outset, the FPAS was developed with **two functions** in mind:

- To identify needs and opportunities for professional development
- To serve as a transparent tool in making decisions with regard to faculty retention, promotion, and rewards.

Components

The FPAS consists of (1) a reviewee-generated record of courses taught, scholarly production, and university and community service; (2) a self-evaluation report on perceived strengths and areas in need of improvement or further development; (3) a detailed course portfolio; (4) a peer review of observed instructional style and content delivery; (5) student evaluations on instructor performance; and (6) a summary review by the department chair geared toward a comprehensive evaluation of the faculty member's performance.

Implementation and Review

The SRC recommended that members of the RQPI-QU reform team conduct a formative evaluation to gauge the success of the FPAS in carrying out its goals. The study was intended to reveal how it was experienced by the stakeholders in the process—specifically, what worked well, what was problematic, and what improvements (if any) the participants wanted to suggest. Its findings were intended to inform future appraisal system deployments.

Findings from the Formative Evaluation

The formative evaluation took place in April 2005, involving group and individual interviews with faculty, department chairs, college deans, and University-level stakeholders. On the condition that the system would be improved, many of the interviewees acknowledged that it had the potential to

- Generate fair and transparent communication between faculty and academic leadership regarding expectations and accomplishments
- Become a tool to assist in recognizing faculty practices that are in need of improvement and in identifying specific areas that merit professional development and support
- Motivate faculty members to perform at ever higher ability levels in those aspects of their jobs in which they are already proficient.

A number of flaws in the initial version generated obstacles to faculty buy-in and contributed to skepticism about the value of performance appraisal. Noteworthy weaknesses included its paper-based format, the inflexibility of some of the evaluation categories, and the inappropriate use of quantitative measures. Nevertheless, many interviewees believed the "culture shock" of systematized accountability and application of universal standards provided a much-needed jolt to those faculty members who were complacent in their positions and regarded themselves as above review.

Final Recommendations

The feedback generated by the formative evaluation is summarized in the following general recommendations:

- Clearly communicate the intended uses of the FPAS to all members of the University community, emphasizing its professional development function.
- Allow the FPAS to be tailored to meet individual college, department, or faculty member profiles.
- Involve the faculty more directly in the process of developing or modifying the appraisal system.
- Shape the system around establishing mutually agreed plans and expectations at the end of one academic year that are revisited and assessed at the conclusion of the next year.
- Simplify the FPAS so it is less complex and less time consuming for reviewees, reviewers, and department heads.
- Revise the evaluation procedures in order to decrease the quantitative emphasis and increase opportunities for open-ended reflections and responses.

These recommendations were fully endorsed by the SRC and the offices responsible for administering the FPAS revised the system accordingly.

Bibliography

Academic Committee, *Documentary File*, University of Qatar, 2000.

Bardach, E., "On Designing Implementable Programs," in G. Majone and E. S. Quade, eds., *Pitfalls of Analysis*, New York: John Wiley & Sons, 1980.

Berman, P., and M. W. McLaughlin, *Federal Programs Supporting Educational Change: Implementing and Sustaining Innovations*, R-1589/8-HEW, Santa Monica, Calif.: RAND Corporation, 1978. As of May 27, 2009:
http://www.rand.org/pubs/reports/R1589.8/

Berman, P., M. W. McLaughlin, G. V. Bass-Golod, E. Pauly, and G. L. Zellman, *Federal Programs Supporting Educational Change: Factors Affecting Implementation and Continuation*, R-1589/7-HEW, Santa Monica, Calif.: RAND Corporation, 1977. As of May 27, 2009:
http://www.rand.org/pubs/reports/R1589.7/

Bikson, Tora K., *Getting it Together: Research and the Real World*, Santa Monica, Calif.: RAND Corporation, P-6447, 1980.

Bikson, Tora K., and John D. Eveland, "Integrating New Tools into Information Work: Technology Transfer as a Framework for Understanding Success," in D. Langford et al., eds., *People and Technology in the Workplace,* Washington D.C.: National Academy Press, 1991.

Bikson, Tora K., Sally Ann Law, Martin Markovich, and Barbara T. Harder, "Facilitating the Implementation of Research Findings: Review, Synthesis, Recommendations," *Proceedings of the Transportation Research Board*, 74th Annual Meeting, Washington, D.C.: National Academy Press, 1995.

Brewer, D. J., C. H. Augustine, G. L. Zellman, G. Ryan, C. A. Goldman, C. Stasz, and L. Constant, *Education for a New Era: Design and Implementation of K–12 Education Reform in Qatar,* MG-548-QATAR, Santa Monica, Calif.: RAND Corporation, 2007. As of May 27, 2009:
http://www.rand.org/pubs/monographs/MG548/

"Bursting at the Seams," *The Peninsula*, January 29, 2008.

Economist Intelligence Unit, *Monthly Country Report, Qatar*, 2008.

Emiri Decree, No. 23, 2004.

Fullan, M., and A. Pomfret, "Research on Curriculum and Instruction Implementation," *Review of Educational Research*, Vol. 47, No. 1, 1977, pp. 335–397.

Guba, E. G., and Y. S. Lincoln, *Effective Evaluation*, San Francisco: Jossey-Bass, 1981.

―――, "Epistemological and Methodological Bases of Naturalistic Inquiry," *Educational Communication and Technology Journal*, Vol. 30, No. 4, 1982, pp. 233–252.

Planning Council, Government of Qatar, 2004 Census, Doha, 2004.

―――, *Labor Market Strategy for the State of Qatar: Main Report*, Volume 1, 2nd Revision, 2005.

Pressman, Jeffrey L., and Aaron Wildavsky, *Implementation: How Great Expectations in Washington are Dashed in Oakland . . .*, second ed., Berkeley: University of California Press, 1979.

Rice, R. E., and E. M. Rogers, "Reinvention in the Innovation Process," *Knowledge*, Vol. 1, No. 4, 1980, pp. 499–514.

Stasz, C., E. R. Eide, and F. Martorell, *Postsecondary Education in Qatar: Employer Demand, Student Choice, and Options for Policy*, MG-644-QATAR, Santa Monica, Calif.: RAND Corporation, 2007. As of May 27, 2009: http://www.rand.org/pubs/monographs/MG644/

Tornatzky, L. G., J. D. Eveland, M. G. Boylan, W. A. Hetzner, E. C. Johnson, D. Roitman, and J. Schneider, *The Process of Technological Innovation: Reviewing the Literature*, Washington, D.C.: National Science Foundation, 1983.

Tornatzky, L. G., E. O. Fergus, J. W. Avellar, and G. W. Fairweather, with M. Fleischer, *Innovation and Social Process*, New York: Pergamon Press, 1980.

Tornatzky, L. G., and E. C. Johnson, "Research on Implementation: Implications for Evaluation Practice and Evaluation Policy," *Evaluation and Program Planning*, Vol. 5, 1982, pp. 193–198.

University Evaluation Committee, *The Qatar University Self Study*, University of Qatar, 2002.

World Bank, *World Development Indicators Online*, online database, 2009. As of May 27, 2009: http://www.worldbank.org/data/onlinedatabases/onlinedatabases.html

Yin, R. K., K. A. Heald, M. E. Vogel, P. D. Fleischauer, and B. C. Vladeck, *A Review of Case Studies of Technological Innovations in State and Local Services*, R-1870-NSF, Santa Monica, Calif.: RAND Corporation, 1976. As of May 27, 2009: http://www.rand.org/pubs/reports/R1870/

Yin, R. K., S. Quick, P. Bateman, and E. Marks, *Changing Urban Bureaucracies: How New Practices Become Routinized—Appendixes*, R-2277-1-NSF, Santa Monica, Calif.: RAND Corporation, 1978. As of May 27, 2009:
http://www.rand.org/pubs/reports/R2277.1/